## SMART QUESTIONS TO ASK
## YOUR INSURANCE AGENT

Today, you can use life insurance to save for your kids' education, to add to your retirement fund, or to ensure the future of your business. When you are dealing with issues of this magnitude, it is your right, as well as your responsibility, to obtain the best possible information for your present and future well-being.

There's no need to let others have control over your financial affairs, to allow anyone else to make decisions for you, or to feel that you are a victim of coercion or circumstance. The purpose of this book is to show how asking questions can improve your insurance savvy, and help you become a comparison shopper. You can become a "questioning detective" and uncover the clues you need to make the best decisions, save money, and get the protection you and your family need.

**Other books in the *Smart Questions* series**

Smart Questions to Ask Your Lawyer
Smart Questions to Ask Your Doctor
*Smart Questions to Ask Your Stockbroker

**Published by
HarperPaperbacks**

*coming soon

# SMART
# QUESTIONS
# TO ASK YOUR
# INSURANCE
# AGENT

## DOROTHY LEEDS

WITH PROFIT AND PENSION PLANNERS, INC.
AND MPPI INSURANCE SERVICES

HarperPaperbacks
*A Division of HarperCollinsPublishers*

HarperPaperbacks    *A Division of* HarperCollins*Publishers*
10 East 53rd Street, New York, N.Y. 10022

Cover illustration by Richard Rossiter

First printing: October 1992

Printed in the United States of America

HarperPaperbacks and colophon are trademarks of
HarperCollins*Publishers*

❖ 10 9 8 7 6 5 4 3 2 1

To Bob Shook: a good friend and an invaluable colleague—the best insurance for success anyone could wish for. Thank-you Bob, for everything.

# ACKNOWLEDGMENTS

Special thank-you's to:
Karen Solem, a great lady and a great editor.
Chris Wilhide, who was always there when we needed her.
Barbara Lowenstein, who made this series possible.
Norman Kurz, for his excellence, kindness, and patience.
Dave Borg, for his professional knowledge and wisdom.
Svjetlana Kabalin, for her devoted administrative assistance.

And a special note of appreciation for Sharyn Kolberg,
whose patience, fortitude, organization, calm demeanor,
and excellent writing skills make it all seem easy.

# CONTENTS

# INTRODUCTION

More than ever, insurance is playing an important part in every family's financial planning. The insurance industry is growing rapidly and expanding its options. We're confronted with myriad decisions and concerns: How much insurance is enough? Is life insurance a good investment? Are all insurance companies the same? How do I know what kind of policy to buy? You don't know . . . unless you *ask questions!*

We need accurate and up-to-date information that goes beyond the usual industry hype. Only by asking careful questions can we begin to get the kind of information we need. However, because the insurance industry is growing so rapidly, it has become increasingly complicated and confusing. There are so many options from which to choose, it's hard to know which ones are right for you. You might feel pressured to make sound financial choices—not just for yourself, but for your family as well.

When you're faced with these difficult choices and are

1

feeling the pressure, you're likely to feel frightened as well; you don't ask as many questions as you should. Consequently, you don't get the information you need.

Yet this is just the time you need all the information you can get. You're probably being asked to make difficult decisions—decisions that may affect the rest of your life, and the lives of your family members as well.

Purchasing life insurance, for instance, used to be a fairly uncomplicated decision. Life insurance served one purpose only: to provide your heirs with financial security in the event of your untimely death. Nowadays, however, you can use life insurance to save for your kids' education, to add to your retirement fund, or to ensure the future of your business. When you are dealing with issues of this magnitude, it is your right, as well as your responsibility, to obtain the best possible information for your present and future well-being.

There's no need to let others have control over your financial affairs, to allow anyone else to make decisions for you, or to feel that you have been coerced or are a victim of circumstance. The purpose of this book is to show how questions can improve your insurance savvy and help you become a comparison shopper. You can become a "questioning detective" and uncover the clues you need to make the best decisions, save you money, and get you the protection you need.

## LEARN TO PROTECT YOURSELF

Successful insurance agents must be well trained in two important aspects of their industry: They must be extremely knowledgeable about the various products they can offer you, and *they must know how to sell.* The more protection you purchase for yourself, your family, and your property, the more money the agent makes.

I don't mean to say that every insurance agent is only out for him or herself, or that agents don't care about their clients. I do mean that in order for you to get the most out of your relationship with your agent, and to get the best, and most appropriate, protection you can afford, you must do more than simply rely on an agent's advice. In order to do that you need to be an "informed consumer" about insurance and about your particular needs and desires.

The problem is that the insurance industry is so complicated, and you're constantly being bombarded with new information. And when you find yourself in a face-to-face situation where you need specific—and vitally important—information, all the facts, figures, advice, and opinions you've heard before fly right out the window. What can you do? How can you find out, right then and there, what you need to know?

You can ask questions.

There are only two ways to get information. One is by watching and reading. The other is by asking questions. You might get some clues about an insurance agent by observing his behavior and personality. You can probably read up on insurance and how it pertains to your situation. This is fine for preparation and background information, but the only way to get immediate information, direct from the source's mouth, and directly applicable to your own problem, is by asking questions.

## WHY DON'T WE ASK MORE?

The reason we don't ask more questions is largely because we're afraid to question authority. We follow the tradition that says, "The insurance agent knows more than I do." We're afraid to doubt his or her advice.

We're reluctant to ask questions because:

- We are afraid we'll be thought stupid if we ask too many questions.
- We assume that agents know more than we do; therefore, we have no right to ask questions.
- We think because we're not buying a large policy, we

shouldn't take up so much time or expect so much attention.
- •We have the impression that insurance agents just want to sell us the largest policy they can.

Insurance agents do have the reputation for over-selling. Good agents have been trained as questioners themselves (unlike some salespeople who have been trained to make a pitch and keep talking until they close the sale). A simple way to tell a good agent is to open the conversation by asking, "What would you recommend?" If the agent tries to sell you a policy without asking you any questions, you should be leery.

Insurance agents know the power of questions and are often questioning experts. This book will provide you with the tools to become a questioning expert yourself and get the information you need.

## BUT WHAT DO I ASK?

Many times we don't ask questions because we're not sure what we should be asking. We figure these people are the experts, they know what they're talking about. "I don't know enough to make this decision myself. My agent is the one who knows all about insurance—and besides, *I don't even know what questions to ask*."

We are faced with difficult decisions every time we seek out financial advice, and often we come away with lingering doubts. "Was there something else I should have asked?" is the haunting refrain most of us have experienced after talking to an insurance agent.

You might wish you had an expert with you to get the necessary information. Well, now you have. This book will turn *you* into the expert. Take it with you when you see your agent. Or write down the pertinent questions that apply to your situation. For example, if you're about to buy a car, concentrate on the section, listed under Property and Casualty, called "Automobile Insurance"; if you're a senior citizen and considering your insurance needs, turn to the section on "Senior Care."

Some of the questions are for you to ask yourself (for instance, when using life insurance as a savings vehicle, you may have to ask yourself if you prefer a conservative approach, or one with more risk but greater growth potential). Some questions are presented for your general knowledge about insurance and help you define terms and concepts. The bulk of the questions are for you to ask your agent.

In writing this book, we set out to explore some of the key issues that are on people's minds. We tried to cover as many areas of insurance as we could. There's no way we could address everyone's individual need for insurance, but we tried to include the most important and most frequently asked questions.

Every question opens up other questions. Add your own questions to the list. We don't presume to have covered every possible insurance situation. But the questions here should get you started, and should stimulate your own questioning process so that you, too, can get the information you really need.

## WHY YOU NEED THIS BOOK
The purpose of this book is threefold:

1. To provide you with the questions to ask in order to get the information you need;
2. To get you into the habit of asking questions; and
3. To build your confidence in dealing with your insurance agent.

After all, the person who asks the questions sets the direction and the topic in a discussion and gains a sense of control in a difficult situation. Most psychologists agree that anxiety arises from loss of control. When you ask a question, the other person feels compelled to answer, and the power goes to the asker. (Just watch the power shift when someone asks you, "Where are you going?" and you answer, "Why do you ask?")

You don't have to take an agent's word for something just because he's an agent, or nod and say yes if you don't understand. You don't have to leave the office until you get a satisfactory answer, no matter how intimidating or aggressive the agent may seem. You have the right to ask questions, and the right to get answers. If an agent won't answer your questions, get someone who will. If an agent says he doesn't have time for explanations, there are other agents around who are willing and able to do so.

## SOME VERY WILLING AGENTS

I was very fortunate, in writing this book, to have found a group of agents who were not only willing and able to answer questions, but to ask them as well.

I worked with six wonderful people from two different firms: Profit and Pension Planners Inc. of Garden City, NY, and MPPI Insurance Services of New York City and Hazlet, NJ.

**Contributors from Profit and Pension Planners Inc. are:**

Michael P. Waters, CLU, ChFC, graduated from the State University of New York at Binghamton in the class of 1984 with a B.A. in political science. He joined Profit and Pension Planners in 1985 and became a member of the firm in 1989. Mr. Waters earned the professional designation of Chartered Life Underwriter and Chartered Financial Consultant from the American College in 1990, one of the youngest people to attain both designations.

Arnold D. Weinstock graduated from the University of Michigan in 1954 with a B.S. in naval architecture and marine engineering. Over the next fourteen years, while a practicing engineer, he pursued graduate studies in industrial management at the Baruch School of CCNY, Hofstra University, and C.W. Post. Mr. Weinstock joined Profit and Pension Planners Inc. in 1967, became a partner in 1972, and owner in 1976. Since then, Profit and Pension Planners has designed and administered over five hundred pension and profit-sharing plans. Mr. Weinstock is currently the pension consultant member of the Executives Association of Greater New York.

Roger J. Schilling graduated from SUNY at Cortland in 1974 with a B.A. in economics. He immediately started his insurance career with the New York Life Insurance Company, spending two years there, followed by two years with the Bank of New York in their Employee Benefit Trust Department. He joined Profit and Pension Planners in 1978 and became a principal of the firm in 1986.

**Contributors from MPPI Insurance Services are:**

Donald Manning, CLU, ChFC, is a principal of MPPI with almost thirty years of experience in all lines of insurance. Mr. Manning holds professional degrees as a Certified Life Underwriter and Chartered Financial Consultant.

Michael A. Kreps, CIC, is vice-president of MPPI and has over twenty years of insurance experience in both personal and commercial lines. He holds a Certified Insurance Counselor professional designation. Mr. Kreps is actively involved in community affairs as both a Boy Scout leader and sponsor and manager of various local team sports.

Robyn S. Reilly is an assistant vice-president of MPPI in charge of their personal lines department. Ms. Reilly has over ten years of exprience in all phases of personal insurance coverages. She is a graduate of the College of Insurance.

These agents and I don't claim to have exhausted all the questions you could, or should, ask about insurance. Nor do we intend to give you specific advice pertaining to your individual circumstances. We have provided questions and examples to give you a basis for comparison: we didn't want to simply provide you with a list of questions, and let it go at that. We wanted you to understand why each of the questions is important, and what you should expect to learn from your agent's answer. When you ask a question, you may want to compare your agent's answer with the one in the book.

## WHERE DO YOU LIVE?

This is one smart question you need to ask yourself as you're reading this book. Although we've tried to answer questions generically, the fact is that insurance laws vary from state to state. If you ask your agent a question from this book, and her answer is different than the one we've provided, the difference may be due to variance in your state law. Once again, *ask* your agent to explain the law to you as it pertains to your home state.

## THE HE/SHE ISSUE

One last word on a technical issue. We did not want to include any gender bias in this book by constantly using "he" to refer to the agent. On the other hand, it is very awkward to use "he/she" and "him or her" throughout. So, when referring to "the agent," we use "he" in some examples and "she" in others.

This is your opportunity to create a new relationship with your insurance agent, and with your prerogatives as an informed consumer. Be an active participant in the most important areas of your life. Insurance agents are there to help you protect your most prized possessions—your health, your life, your home, your material assets. You have the right to a clear and comprehensive understanding of everything that affects you. Make sure you stand up for that right, and start asking smart questions.

# SMART QUESTIONS TO ASK WHEN CHOOSING AN INSURANCE AGENT AND AN INSURANCE COMPANY

There is one question you may want to ask before you begin reading this book, and that is: *What is insurance, anyway?* To understand the concept of insurance, picture a colonial village in Virginia. Ten or fifteen families have settled here: built their homes, cleared their land, and planted crops. At a town meeting one evening, someone suggests that it would be a tragedy if one of the homes accidentally caught fire or was destroyed by flood or hurricane. Wouldn't it be a good idea if each family chipped in some money each year to form a common fund so that in the event one or more of them suffered a loss, they could rebuild the lost homesteads? Those too poor to afford to donate money might pledge furniture or tools or offer plowing, planting, or harvesting services in lieu of a monetary contribution to the fund.

9

This accumulation of money, goods, and services in a common pool for the benefit of the participants is called insurance. As the number of participants in the pool grew, and the types of risks to be guarded against became more complex, goods and services were dropped from the pool, and money became the means for replacing the economic losses suffered by participants.

## INSURANCE COMPANIES AND INSURANCE POLICIES

As the pool of money and participants continued to grow, it became necessary to hire people to manage the money: collect it, invest it, keep track of all the transactions, and pay it out against the claim of the pool participants. Gradually, the pool managers became independent groups known as insurance companies.

These insurance companies then began to issue insurance policies. An insurance policy is a legal agreement between the insurance company and the pool participant (or the "insured") which spells out what the company will do in the event of an insured-against loss—how much the insured will be paid if a loss is suffered, in what manner the payment will be made, and when, and how much the cost for this protection might be. The cost is usually stated as "premium" payable over some definite time period and at some agreed-upon frequency (annually, semiannually, quarterly, or monthly).

All guarantees and promises are spelled out in the policy, also known as the insurance contract, so that each party, the insured and the insurance company, knows where it stands.

## THE INSURANCE AGENT

Nowadays, you usually obtain insurance through an insurance agent. An insurance agent is your consultant and adviser. He helps you to clarify your needs and helps you to satisfy them by choosing the proper policy.

One of the most important questions you must ask

before you shop for an insurance agent is this: How can I choose an insurance agent who will truly represent me and not be primarily concerned with how much commission he makes?

Ask your friends, neighbors, and even business competitors for references. Ask questions about how comfortable they are with their present agent, what kind of service they get, what problems they have encountered, and how professional the agency is.

An agent should be accessible, return your calls promptly, answer all your questions, make suggestions, act professionally, be able to handle all your specific needs, and represent quality companies.

A good agent will try to put herself in your position and present to you the solutions she would consider if she were you. She should give you options to consider now, and in the future. She should not be suggesting policies you cannot afford, or trying to sell you more than you need.

Some considerations might be: Does the agent cut you off in midsentence, or does she let you finish your thought before responding? Does the agent take other telephone calls while in a meeting with you, or does he devote complete attention to you? Does the agent have set answers for each problem you explain, or does he offer several options for you to choose? Does the agent try to dominate the relationship, or does he let you have some input? Often a "gut" reaction about an agent is correct; if he seems to be too busy to focus on your problems, maybe this is not the agent for you.

The only way you can find out if an agent is right for you is by asking questions. You may not choose to ask the agent all of the questions in this section. But you do want to ask enough questions to get the information you need. You also want to find out how willing this agent is to answer any questions you might have, and how you react to this agent's manner and attitudes.

A good agent wants to be sure you understand what you're getting, what is and what isn't covered, and how much it will cost. If the agent is reluctant to answer any of your questions, find another agent. Choosing an agent, like choosing a doctor, a lawyer, or any other professional, is a very important decision; if an agent does not understand your need to ask questions, then perhaps you should look somewhere else.

# CHOOSING AN AGENT

## THE BASICS

### ARE THERE DIFFERENT TYPES OF INSURANCE AGENTS?

Insurance agents usually come in three categories: independent agents, captive agents, and exclusive agents.

Independent agents are self-employed, represent more than one company, and are free to sell many forms and types of insurance.

Captive agents, while also self-employed, operate their business under the guidelines and direction of the single company they represent. You would deal with that agent for the initial placement of your business. After that, you deal directly with the insurance company.

Exclusive agents represent one company, and are employees of that company.

### AM I BETTER OFF ECONOMICALLY BUYING FROM ONE TYPE OF AGENT THAN ANOTHER?

Not necessarily. You should consider a number of factors when buying insurance. These factors will rank in different order from individual to individual and business to business. Here are a few of the factors that should be considered:

*Price:* Some people consider this the only criterion. That is far from true. When you buy insurance, you are buying an entire philosophy. You could shortchange yourself if you use this as your only criterion.

*Coverage:* What protection are you actually buying? If you are making a comparison between two policies, you need to know what they both cover, and what they both don't cover. As long as you are comparing equals, you can make a good decision as to which policy is the best for you.

*Stability:* In today's "shaky" economy, with many financial institutions experiencing difficulties—including banks, real estate, and stock-brokerage firms—the stability of the insurance company should be considered. Has the company been around a long time? Does it have a rating from one of the insurance rating organizations (Best's, Moody's, etc.)?

*Claims-Paying Ability:* What is the company's reputation for paying claims? How fast are they paid? How much paperwork is involved?

*Agent Representative:* Does the agent possess the skills and knowledge that today's products, time, and conditions demand? Does he believe in continuing education? Does he keep up with the times? Does he operate a professional office? Is he willing to explain what you don't understand? Is he too loud? Too quiet? Too pushy? Too indecisive?

These are not necessarily the only conditions you should consider, but merely a sampling. You can, and should, add your own ingredients to make a perfect match. The most important criterion is a comfortable blend of all of the above. Choose your insurance representative as you would choose any other professional. The bottom line is that you want to deal with someone that you feel comfortable talking to and working with—someone that you trust.

## WHAT SHOULD I EXPECT FROM AN AGENT ONCE I DECIDE ON ONE?

No matter how much money your agent is (or isn't) making from your commission, you should be able to call him periodically to ask questions. If there is anything you don't understand, or if you want a brief outline of your policy, you should feel free to ask him. If you find that your agent is not responsive, and doesn't return your phone calls, it's time to find another agent.

Keep in mind that commissions on property and casualty insurance (homeowners, automobile, commercial property, etc.) are much lower than those for life and health insurance. An average commission might be 15 percent of the premiums you pay. If your premium is $300 a year and your agent is earning $45 a year, it would be unprofitable for that agent to visit you two times a year and handle all your correspondence, mail, etc. However, most agents will be glad to give you the phone service you require.

If your agent is making several hundred dollars a year from your business, you probably should expect a once-yearly visit from the agent or an annual review.

## HOW INCONVENIENT IS IT TO CHANGE AGENTS IF I'M NOT SATISFIED WITH THE ONE I'VE GOT?

There should be no inconvenience involved. A new agent might ask you to send her copies of your old policies. You should keep the originals in a file and be able to duplicate them easily. The new agent will not usually need the whole policy, just the printed matter on the first few pages. The rest is what they call boilerplate, or standard form.

You might even be better off starting from scratch with

the new agent—there might be things that the old agent missed and you don't want to duplicate his mistakes.

## IF I'M INTERESTED IN SWITCHING AGENTS, HOW AND WHEN SHOULD I SHOP FOR NEW INSURANCE?

The best time to shop around for new insurance is a month to two months prior to the expiration date on your existing policies. If you cancel prior to the expiration date, other than for nonpayment of premium, you will have short-rate charges built into the cancellation. That means if you go elsewhere in midterm, be prepared to spend additional monies over the normal pro rata costs for the insurance.

For instance, if your policy costs $120 a year and you cancel after six months, the normal pro rata cost would be $60. If you decide to cancel midterm and move to another agent, be prepared to pay an additional 10 percent on the unearned premium. In the example above, it would be six dollars. If you have a large policy and you have a lot of time left to go on it, you could be paying several hundred dollars.

## Questions to Ask the Agent

## HOW LONG HAVE YOU BEEN IN THE BUSINESS?

You probably want to go with someone who's been in the business for at least three to five years—sufficient time to have gained practical experience. You want to know that this agent is going to be around down the line, should you ever have questions or difficulties with your policies.

## CAN I HAVE THE NAMES AND PHONE NUMBERS OF A FEW OF YOUR CURRENT CLIENTS TO CALL FOR REFERENCES?

This may be the best method of finding out if an agent is competent. Ask him for several client references and call them to determine whether or not they are satisfied with the insurance policies and with the service they get from this agent.

## CAN I HAVE A LIST OF INSURANCE COMPANIES YOU REPRESENT?

If two or three are rated as top carriers in the country, then chances are these companies have scrutinized the agent before they've allowed him to sell their products. Agents are required to do a certain amount of business with a company in order to maintain their status as representatives of that company; so you know he's doing a fair amount of his business with quality companies.

## HOW DO YOU GET PAID?

If an insurance agent won't tell you how he or she gets paid, you should probably look for another agent. Some agents get paid on salary, some by commission. Any good agent will tell you about salary and commissions if you ask. One is not necessarily better than the other, but if you suspect an agent is trying to sell you more insurance than you need (in order to make a higher commission), it may be easier for you to judge if you know the answer to this question.

## DO YOU HAVE ANY ADVANCED TRAINING OR QUALIFICATIONS AS AN INSURANCE AGENT?

All insurance agents have to be licensed by the state. Licensing exams in most states are comprehensive and difficult. If an agent has been in business for several years, and/or comes highly recommended to you, it's probably not important that he has advanced training or designations.

It's not necessary to be a CLU (Chartered Life Underwriter) to be a good life-insurance agent, and it doesn't guarantee competence or reliability. But it does show a certain amount of seriousness and professional achievement. And it does indicate a large fund of knowledge. A property and casualty agent might be designated a CIC (Certified Insurance Consultant) or CPU (Commercial Property Underwriter).

Professional designations are signs that the agent has kept abreast of the changes in the insurance industry and is making insurance a professional career. However, it is more important that your agent is knowledgeable about current laws and regulations and has quality insurance companies behind him.

## WHEN DID YOU GET YOUR LAST DESIGNATION? HAVE YOU TAKEN ANY COURSES LATELY?

You want to ascertain whether or not this agent is familiar with the latest changes and current regulations. If she hasn't taken any courses, ask her how she does keep up with industry changes.

# CHOOSING AN INSURANCE COMPANY

## THE BASICS

### HOW DO I KNOW WHICH ARE QUALITY INSURANCE COMPANIES?

One way to find out is by checking in Best's Insurance Reports, Moody's, or Standard & Poor's. These guides provide rating systems for insurance companies. You can usually find them in the library. Your state insurance department might also have this information.

Best's gives each company a letter rating, from A-plus to C-minus and nonrated, with A-plus being the best. The letter rating indicates the insurer's financial stability. There is a second, Roman-numeral rating, which indicates the financial size of the company. The highest rating is XV(15).

Moody's and Standard & Poor's also rate most of the larger property and casualty insurance companies. The ratings are usually from AAA to C, with AAA being the best. Be sure to check the glossary of terms and guidelines in each system so that you understand how each of them works.

## DOES THE COMPANY HAVE FINANCIAL STABILITY?

Besides checking one of the rating guides, you can also obtain a particular company's annual report. You can read it or discuss the report with your accountant and determine whether the company is financially solid.

## WHAT ELSE SHOULD I BE LOOKING FOR IN AN INSURANCE COMPANY?

One of the key items to look for is that the insurance company is approved and licensed in your state. If it is, there is usually a guarantee fund that would pay you or cover your claims and refund any premiums should that company go out of business. If you're buying insurance from an excess (unlicensed) carrier in your state, you will have no protection if that carrier goes bankrupt or pulls out of your state.

## HOW DO I KNOW WHICH COMPANY IS RIGHT FOR ME?

This is a question only you and your agent can answer. If you understand your particular business and/or personal insurance needs, match up the company that suits you best. For instance, several companies have special programs for specific businesses, such as beauty salons, metal workers, even Chinese restaurants. In the personal area, is the insurance company willing to cover high-value fine arts or jewelry, if that's what you need to insure?

Make a "wish list" before you go to see your agent. Write down everything you'd like to have covered, and then ask your agent to help you determine which company would best fulfill your needs.

## DOES THE COMPANY HAVE A SOLID PROVEN REPUTATION FOR CLAIMS HANDLING AND DO THEY HANDLE THE CLAIMS FAIRLY AND PROMPTLY?

Ask your agent for references of people who have had claims with this company. Ask them how the claims were handled, if they had any problems, if they felt they were treated courteously and paid promptly. You can also consult consumer magazines, such as *Consumer Reports,* for comparisons among different companies.

## DOES THE COMPANY DEMONSTRATE A COMMITMENT TO SERVICE THROUGH HIGHLY TRAINED EMPLOYEES?

You can determine this either by looking at the company's annual report or asking your agent about the backgrounds of the company's employees.

## ARE THERE DIFFERENT KINDS OF LIFE-INSURANCE COMPANIES?

There are two basic types of life-insurance companies: stock companies, and mutual companies.

## WHAT IS A STOCK COMPANY?

This type of insurance company is owned by stockholders, the same way General Motors is owned by stockholders. You can buy shares of stock in such insurance companies through your stockbroker, and you need not buy a policy to do so. You buy the stock as an investment, just like any other stock. The dividends declared by the company are paid to the stockholders, not the policyholders.

## WHAT IS A MUTUAL COMPANY?

You don't buy stock from a mutual company, you buy insurance policies. The policyholders own the company. When you buy a policy from a mutual company, you become a "part owner" of that company.

The profits of the company are paid to the policy owners in the form of dividends. These dividends can be used to pay your premiums or to buy more insurance, can be left in the policy to grow at interest just like a mini–bank account, or can be taken out as cash.

## ARE THERE OTHER DIFFERENCES BETWEEN STOCK AND MUTUAL COMPANIES?

In general, the premium rates offered by stock companies are lower than those offered by mutual companies. Because mutual companies earn dividends, however, you may end up paying lower rates over the long term.

Look at the chart below, which shows premium rates for three males, ages thirty-five, forty, and forty-five. You'll see on line one that the thirty-five-year-old is paying $8.26 for each $1,000 of life insurance he's purchased from a stock company. If he purchased the same amount of insurance from a mutual company, he would be paying a higher premium (minus whatever dividends he received) initially: $9.13. But after twenty years of receiving dividends, the cost of his premiums has averaged out to $4.53. So in the long run, the premiums for the mutual-company policy cost less.

| Age | Stock Company Premium: $/1,000 | Mutual Company Avg.:$/1,000* | Avg.: $/1,000** |
|-----|-------------------------------|------------------------------|-----------------|
| 35  | $ 8.26                        | $ 9.13                       | $ 4.53          |
| 40  | 10.84                         | 11.53                        | 5.92            |
| 45  | 14.26                         | 14.45                        | 7.65            |

\* Initial premium less average dividend over 10 years
\** Initial premium less average dividend over 20 years

## ARE THERE OTHER DIFFERENCES THAT ARE IMPORTANT?

Probably the most clear-cut difference is that the cash values (see the section on life insurance for a full explanation of cash values) build up higher and faster in mutual companies' policies than in stock companies' policies. There are exceptions, of course, so keep your agent on his toes.

In the same comparison of policies above, the cash value buildup in these policies looks like this, after ten years and twenty years:

| | Stock Company | | Mutual Company | |
|---|---|---|---|---|
| Age | $/1,000 10 yrs. | $/1,000 20 yrs. | Avg.: $/1,000 | Avg.: $/1,000 |
| 35 | $55 | $71 | $ 95 | $236 |
| 40 | 75 | 220 | 117 | 285 |
| 45 | 101 | 278 | 145 | 341 |

## HOW DO YOU ACCOUNT FOR THESE DIFFERENCES?

When stock companies make money on their investments, they are obliged to pay out dividends to their stockholders, whereas mutual companies can earmark more dollars to increasing both the earning rate of the policy cash values as well as the dividends paid to the policyholder.

## WHAT ARE DIRECT WRITERS?

Certain companies are called direct writers because you deal directly with the company. They employ sales agents to sell their products, but the agents do not handle premiums or claims. They are also limited in the sense that they can sell only those products their company offers. Direct-writer policies are geared to the "usual" risk and they are generally unable to offer customized coverage such as coverage for expensive jewelry, high-value cars, or specialized coverages for businesses.

## I'VE HEARD THE TERMS "POLICY," "CONTRACT," AND "PRODUCT" USED IN REFERRING TO INSURANCE. WHAT DO THEY MEAN?

Essentially, they all mean the same thing. An insurance contract and an insurance policy are one and the same.

An insurance policy may also be referred to as a product sold by the insurance company.

## CHOOSING A POLICY

### INSURANCE POLICIES ALWAYS SEEM TERRIBLY COMPLICATED. HOW DO I READ MY POLICY SO THAT IT MAKES SENSE TO ME?

Most people find it difficult to read through an entire policy. Many of the policies are currently written in so-called layman's terms; however, they are still difficult to interpret.

Policies usually contain three or four different sections. The first is usually the declarations section, which indicates who the named insured is, the policy dates, and the limits of coverage that are applicable to your type of business or home. The first thing you should do is check that the name, address, and location are correct. Then check that the dates of coverage are correct. Finally, check the typed-in sections that indicate how much coverage is included in this policy.

Another section in your policy will define what is covered. This section often contains language that is difficult to understand. Be sure to ask your agent to explain anything that does not make sense to you.

The important part of the insurance policy to read is the exclusions. This section tells you exactly what is *not* covered under this policy. If you know what is excluded under your policy, you'll know if you need to get extra protection for your particular needs.

### WHAT DO I LOOK FOR WHEN COMPARING COVERAGES UNDER DIFFERENT COMPANIES' POLICIES?

It is important to look at quality of coverage as well as price when shopping for insurance. All policies are not alike and coverages vary greatly. For instance, some companies cover backup of sewers and drains as part of their homeowners coverage, some do not. This may be important to you if you live in a low-lying area.

Remember to look at the coverages *and* the exclusions (things that are not covered) and limitations (dollar amounts) in a policy to determine what you are actually getting. When shopping for a new car, you look at the features as well as the price. Shop for insurance the same way.

## IS IT EVER SMART TO BUY THE LEAST EXPENSIVE POLICY?

Some coverages, like workers' compensation and disability benefits, are fairly standard. In those cases, if you can get a discount off the manual rates, the answer might be yes. In the case of a homeowners policy or a business-owners policy, it's important to look at all the other factors discussed above.

It's important that the agent you deal with be up front with you and tell you this is a "Rolls-Royce" type policy, this is a "Cadillac," and this is a "Chevrolet"—you can make your own decision based on your personal preferences and your financial status.

## CAN I PAY MY PREMIUMS IN INSTALLMENTS?

This is a question to ask your agent about the particular policy you're buying. Most insurance companies will send you an annual bill and ask you if you want to pay it in total, or pay in three, six, or twelve installments. There is a service fee for paying in installments (usually about 3 or 4 percent).

Insurance companies sometimes allow you to pay premiums with your credit card. But if you do, you'll be paying anywhere from 16 to 20 percent, depending on what your card charges, instead of the nominal interest fee from the insurance company.

## SUPPOSE I DECIDE I WANT TO CANCEL MY POLICY. WHAT DOCUMENTS WILL I NEED?

You should send your original policy back to your agent by certified or registered mail. If you've lost your original policy, or do not want to send it back, there is a cancellation notice form. You should also include a letter indicating that you want to cancel, outlining the company, the policy number, the dates of coverage, the date you wish to cancel, and the reason you want to cancel.

## WHAT HAPPENS IF MY INSURANCE COMPANY GOES OUT OF BUSINESS?

Call your agent and ask him to explain the problem situation to you. It may be that the company has not gone out of business entirely, but is not writing any more business in your state. In that case your policy will be good until expiration date, at which time your agent can replace it with another policy.

The insurance company might stop doing business with your agent. In that case you'll get a notification of cancellation indicating that the agent no longer represents that company. Again, call your agent and review the situation with her. Ask if she can replace your coverage with a similar company, or if she can recommend another agent that is still writing business with that company.

If your insurance company does go out of business in your state and is not a licensed insurance company, and you have claims that are pending, get in touch with your attorney immediately. If the company goes out of business and there are no claims, contact your agent immedi-

ately to replace your insurance coverage. Chances are if
the company is not licensed in the state, you will not get
any refunded premiums.

## IS THERE ANYPLACE I CAN CALL IF I HAVE BASIC INSURANCE QUESTIONS?

You can call the National Insurance Consumer Helpline
at 800-942-4242. The Helpline operates from 8:00 A.M. to
8:00 P.M. Eastern Time, Monday through Friday. Trained
personnel and licensed insurance agents can answer
questions and/or send you materials about how to
choose an agent or insurance company, and about auto,
health, home, and life insurance. They can also direct
complaints to appropriate sources.

SECTION 2

# SMART QUESTIONS TO ASK ABOUT HEALTH INSURANCE (with Michael Waters)

Human beings are incredibly resilient. We often bounce back from a serious illness none the worse for the wear and go on with our lives as if nothing had happened.

Humans are also frail and fragile creatures. Despite our best efforts and precautions, and despite the fantastic advances in medical research and diagnosis, we can become seriously ill at any time.

Illness can often be very frightening. The situation can be compounded if you are faced with the prospect of expensive medical bills and possible loss of time and wages from work. Owning a medical-insurance policy can help with these concerns, both financially and emotionally.

Medical insurance may be the most necessary and least understood of all insurance that you should have. If you're purchasing insurance on your own, there are a huge variety of plans available—many of which are expensive and don't provide the kind of coverage you need. If insurance is provided through your place of employment, it is often complex and confusing.

During the last few years health-insurance costs have skyrocketed, rising by an average of 35 to 40 percent *a year* for many insurance clients. These dramatic leaps in rates (as compared with previous 5-to-15-percent increases) have led many insurance companies to create and market new and innovative policies to try to help control the cost of health care. However, this makes it even more difficult to choose the policy that is just right for you.

Therefore, it is more important than ever that you get as much information as you can before you make any purchasing decisions. You want to know exactly what is, and is not, being covered by any policy, and what your available options are. Only by asking the right questions can you be assured that you will receive the maximum benefit from any plan you choose.

# HEALTH INSURANCE

## THE BASICS

### WHY DO I NEED MEDICAL INSURANCE?

No one wants to be sick. We all want to be able to take care of ourselves and our families. Unfortunately, sooner or later we all get sick and require some form of medical treatment—which may prove to be extremely costly.

It's also an unfortunate fact of life in this country that you may not be able to get the treatment you need without health insurance. Some doctors and hospital emergency rooms have turned patients away because they didn't have insurance. Over 37 million Americans today do not have health insurance—and for many of them that means they do not have adequate medical care.

Your life may be at stake when you make health-insurance decisions. You must be well informed to get the best coverage for you and your family. In order to do this, you must ask questions, and continue asking until you are satisfied with the answers you get.

## WHERE DO I OBTAIN MEDICAL INSURANCE?

There are several different ways of obtaining medical insurance. Many people obtain medical insurance through their place of employment. Most large companies and trade unions provide medical coverage to their workers.

The next best place to obtain health insurance is directly from your insurance agent or through your local Blue Cross or Blue Shield office. However, purchasing an individual or family policy this way can be very expensive. Also, if you have significant health problems, you may find it difficult to find anyone who will insure you.

Another place you may obtain insurance is through a club, organization, or association to which you belong, such as AARP (American Association of Retired Persons) or NAFE (National Association of Female Executives), religious groups, and professional and civic organizations such as a bar association or fraternal organization. These policies often offer lower deductibles and more comprehensive benefits than individually purchased policies, but you must be careful that the coverage being offered is what you really need.

## WHAT TYPES OF HEALTH INSURANCE ARE AVAILABLE TODAY?

There are basically three different types of insurance available to you (and some companies allow you to choose from a menu of all three): "traditional" health insurance, health maintenance organizations (HMOs), and preferred provider organizations (PPOs).

## WHAT IS "TRADITIONAL" HEALTH INSURANCE?

This type of insurance is broken down into three categories: basic medical (better known as Hospitalization), medical/surgical, and major medical.

## WHAT ARE HOSPITALIZATION AND MEDICAL/SURGICAL?

Hospitalization covers the cost of your hospital stay—within limitations. The insurance company only covers a limited number of days in the hospital and will only pay an amount that they have previously determined for each day—no matter what the actual cost of a day's stay in the hospital. Probably the most well-known basic medical benefit plan is Blue Cross hospitalization. A typical hospitalization plan from Blue Cross will cover the first 120 days in the hospital each calendar year providing you use a hospital that participates in the Blue Cross program (most hospitals do).

Medical/surgical is really part of your hospitalization coverage—the part that pertains to the actual services of the doctors involved—the surgeon, the anesthesiologist, the physical therapist, etc. It usually also covers specified surgeries done on an outpatient basis.

This type of insurance typically covers (totally or partially):

- room and board (private rooms are paid for only when there is a medical need for one)
- medical supplies (drugs and equipment provided by hospital personnel)

- •routine nursing care
- •use of the operating room, recovery room, etc.
- •doctor bills as specified in the policy
- •food

## WHAT ARE SOME TYPICAL RESTRICTIONS OR LIMITATIONS IN BASIC MEDICAL COVERAGE?

Hospitalization and medical/surgical may not cover all of the expenses of your hospital stay, and may have certain requirements that you must meet before you can be covered. Some of the things to look for are:

- •Second Opinion: Your policy may require that you have a second opinion before you have any non-emergency surgery.
- •Admission Requirements: Your policy may state that whenever possible you must be admitted on the morning of your scheduled surgery, as opposed to the night before. The insurance company wants to pay for the least amount of days possible.
- •Outpatient Requirements: Minor surgery may have to be performed on an outpatient basis (you go into the hospital or doctor's office, have the procedure done, and return home all in the same day). Recovery time is spent at home.
- •Waiting Period: Some policies may state that you must be hospitalized for a specified number of days before they will begin coverage. For example, your policy may say that your coverage begins only on the third day of hospitalization. That means you are responsible for any and all charges incurred on the first two days.
- •Maximum Coverage: Be sure that the dollar amount of coverage provided is realistic for the number of days the policy allows you to stay in the hospital.

For instance, a policy may say it covers 100 days of hospitalization—or a maximum dollar coverage of $20,000. If you are in the hospital for 100 days, you'll probably run up a bill larger than $20,000, and you'll be responsible for the rest.

## WHAT IS MAJOR MEDICAL?

Major medical covers specified doctors' bills not incurred during hospitalization or surgical procedures, and can be purchased separately or as a package with hospitalization. These plans generally require you to submit medical bills, which after review, are reimbursed to you.

## HOW CAN I BE SURE THAT MY COVERAGES DON'T OVERLAP AND THAT I DON'T HAVE MORE COVERAGE THAN I NEED?

Many people have more than one health-insurance policy. You don't want to pay for coverage you already have elsewhere. Anytime you're purchasing new insurance, be sure you have all of your existing policies with you. If necessary, make a list of everything that's covered on your existing policy, and everything the new policy is offering. Compare lists and ask questions if there are overlapping areas. If there's any portion of a policy you don't understand, have your agent explain it to you fully.

## WHAT IS AN HMO?

HMO stands for Health Maintenance Organization. Your premiums to the HMO cover all or most of your health-care needs. There may be no further charges at all, or you may be charged a nominal fee of a few dollars.

When you become a member of an HMO, you must use only the doctors and health facilities authorized by that HMO (except for emergency situations).

## WHAT IS A PPO?

PPO stands for Preferred Provider Organization. A PPO is formed when your association, employer, or your insurance company contracts specific doctors, hospitals, and health-care workers to provide their services to members at a discount cost. They are paid a monthly fee for each person they service under the plan.

Once again, your choice of physician and facility are limited to those participating in the PPO plan.

## WHAT ARE THE SIMILARITIES BETWEEN HMOs AND PPOs?

Both HMOs and PPOs come in two basic forms. The first type is termed a group or staff model. The setup is similar to a medical clinic, but with a variety of medical-care practitioners available only to subscribers to the health plan. The second type, called an individual practice association, consists of independent physicians who practice in their own offices and see plan members there.

## WHAT ARE THE DIFFERENCES BETWEEN HMOs AND PPOs?

There are three big differences between PPOs and HMOs. The first is in how the participating physician is paid: HMOs generally pay their physicians a monthly fee no matter how many patients they see, as if they were on salary. PPOs pay their practitioners on a fee-for-service basis; they are paid only for patients they actually see.

The second difference is that HMOs are required to be registered with the federal government and meet certain qualifications, while PPOs are not.

The third difference is that more often than not, PPOs are associated with traditional insurance plans sold by insurance companies. An association will usually offer its members (or a company its employees) a choice of XYZ Insurance Company's traditional insurance plan, or XYZ Insurance Company's PPO plan. This is called a freedom or point-of-service plan. HMOs are stand-alone plans, not necessarily offered in conjunction with an insurance company's traditional plan.

## WHAT ARE SOME ADVANTAGES AND DISADVANTAGES OF HMOs AND PPOs?

The major advantage is cost. Both HMOs and PPOs provide health care at substantially lower costs. However, you are giving up freedom of choice when you sign on with these plans. You should also be concerned about what happens if you have nonemergency medical problems and you are in another city or state and cannot get to a participating doctor or hospital.

## WHAT SHOULD I FIND OUT ABOUT AN HMO OR PPO BEFORE I JOIN?

HMOs and PPOs can be very good deals. As with any good deal, however, you must ask questions to be sure that what you are getting will cover all your needs. Questions you should be asking include:

- Who are the doctors involved in the plan, and what are their credentials?

- What hospital(s) or other health care facilities are covered under this plan?
- What do I do in an emergency?
- If this is clinic-type set up, will I see the same doctor every time I come?
- Are there any restrictions to this coverage? Exactly what is and is not covered under this plan?

## SMART QUESTIONS ABOUT COVERAGE

### WHAT DOES MY MEDICAL INSURANCE COVER?

This question should be asked no matter what type of plan you're considering—HMO, PPO, or traditional coverage. Medical-insurance policies vary widely from company to company and even within different policies from the same company. It is very important to consult your benefit booklet (which comes with your policy) or insurance expert to find out exactly what your policy covers. This is especially important when you are considering purchasing or changing policies; the only way you can comparison-shop is if you ask specifically what is covered by each policy you are considering.

### WHAT DOESN'T MY MEDICAL PLAN COVER?

This is perhaps the more appropriate question to ask. When looking at a medical policy, look for the section entitled "Exclusions." This will tell you what areas are *not* covered under this insurance contract. Some typical exclusions are:

- preexisting conditions (a medical condition which you had prior to purchasing the policy, such as a high-school football injury or a history of migraine headaches). Each policy has different restrictions on preexisting conditions. Some policies will not cover charges related to preexisting conditions at all. Some policies will pay after a certain time limit passes without a flare-up of this condition. Many insurance companies will simply refuse to insure you at all on the basis of certain preexisting conditions.

- preventive care, meaning routine physical exams and testing
- injuries caused while committing a felony
- attempted suicide
- psychiatric care
- dental costs
- cosmetic surgery

## HOW ARE MY INSURANCE COSTS DETERMINED?

There are several factors that go into individual insurance costs, including your age, your health history, whether or not you smoke, how many people are covered under the policy, and your gender.

## MY INSURANCE POLICY HAS A $300 DEDUCTIBLE. WHAT IS A DEDUCTIBLE, AND TO WHAT CHARGES DOES IT APPLY?

The first medical bills each year are not covered until you pay a specified amount out of your pocket. That is called the deductible.

If your medical plan has a deductible of $300, it means that before any bills are reimbursed by the insurance company, you must pay $300 out of your pocket.

Not all deductibles are charted annually. There are medical plans where the deductible applies to each separate illness. These are called "per cause" deductibles.

This type of plan can be very expensive if your health is poor in a given year.

## DOES EACH MEMBER OF MY FAMILY HAVE TO MEET A SEPARATE DEDUCTIBLE?

This is an important consideration when choosing a medical plan. Some plans require each person to meet their own deductible. Other programs will limit a family to two or three deductibles.

The best type of family limit is called a "sugarbowl" deductible, which limits the family to an overall dollar maximum. A sugarbowl deductible limit can keep your family's bout with the flu from becoming a financial hardship. A friend of mine has eight children, who have a tendency to come down with simultaneous illnesses. The initial deductible on his medical plan is $500, with a family limit of $1,500. Without this limit, he would have to pay a $4,000 deductible, or $500 for each of his children.

## DOES MY HEALTH INSURANCE PAY FOR THE TOTAL COST OF COVERED PROCEDURES?

Maybe, but probably not. Most policies require the policyholder to pay a deductible and then participate in a cost-sharing program called coinsurance. In a nutshell, this means that the insurance company only covers a percent of your medical bills. For example, the insurance company may cover 80 percent of your bills after the deductible. You are responsible for the remaining 20 percent.

Many policies, however, limit the out-of-pocket expense you can incur. A policy may pay 80 percent of your medical bills (after the deductible has been met) and require you to pay 20 percent until you have paid $2,500 out of your own pocket. After that, the insurance company will pay 100 percent of your medical bills.

Coinsurance can be for the whole policy or for specific parts such as private-duty nursing or psychiatric benefits. All policies are different, so it is essential to understand this portion of your policy, and ask your insurance company or agent to explain exactly how coinsurance works in your policy.

## HOW DO THE DEDUCTIBLE AND COINSURANCE WORK TOGETHER?

The best way to understand this is to construct an example:

| | |
|---|---|
| Your deductible is: | $300 |
| Your coinsurance is: | 80/20 on first $2,500 in bills |
| Your medical bills are: | $13,000 for the year |

You would pay the first $300 as the deductible. That leaves $12,700 to be covered by insurance. The insurance company then covers 80 percent of the next $2,500 in bills, or $2,000, and you pay 20 percent, or $500. This leaves $10,200 out of the original $13,000 due, which the insurance company pays in full. In this example the insurance company paid $12,200 and you paid $800 ($300 deductible plus $500 coinsurance).

## WILL MY MEDICAL EXPENSES BE COVERED NO MATTER WHAT THE DOCTOR CHARGES?

This is an important question to ask, because there are several different ways insurance companies have to determine how much they will pay for a particular service.

Many plans pay benefits according to what the usual charge for a procedure in your area is; if your doctor charges more than that, you'll have to pay the difference yourself. Other plans pay benefits according to a predetermined schedule. That way you would know in advance how your doctor's fees compare with what the insurance company will allow.

Most policies nowadays pay claims based on a schedule referred to as "reasonable and customary." A reasonable charge is whatever the insurance company says it is. These schedules are very often arbitrary and capricious, so it is very important to make sure that your doctor's fees are in line with your insurance company's schedule.

## HOW DO I FIND OUT IF MY DOCTOR'S FEES ARE "IN LINE"?

Many insurance companies offer a service called pretreatment review. Pretreatment review provides you with an 800 number to call and have contemplated treatment reviewed for cost and necessity. In fact, some insurance companies make this mandatory.

Before you have any procedure done, ask the doctor how much it will cost. Then call your insurance company and find out how much they normally pay for such a procedure. Sometimes the insurance company and the doctor can work out a compromise beforehand so that you can get your necessary medical care without having to worry about whether or not the costs will be covered.

## CAN I ARGUE WITH THE INSURANCE COMPANY'S DEFINITION OF "REASONABLE"? IF SO, HOW DO I GO ABOUT IT?

If you think that the insurance company is being unreasonable, the first thing to do is contact your insurance agent (or your employee representative at work). Have them take up your case with the company.

If for some reason your agent is not available, you can contact the claims department of your insurance company. They may ask you to get a letter from your doctor explaining his charges, or they may contact the doctor themselves.

## WHAT IS THE MAXIMUM BENEFIT UNDER THE POLICY?

Health-insurance policies have maximum benefits that range from as little as $50,000 to as high as unlimited. Ten years ago a policy with a one-million-dollar maximum lifetime benefit was considered an unlimited policy. The medical advances in the last decade, along with the corresponding elevation in fees, have now made it entirely possible to reach the million-dollar maximum. Of course, the higher the maximum benefit, the higher the cost of your policy.

## ARE THERE ANY MAXIMUMS ON SPECIFIC PROVISIONS OF MY POLICY?

Medical procedures that have a tendency to be overused generally set monetary limits, or limit the number of visits that will be covered. For example, chiropractic coverage may be limited to fifty visits a year under some policies or a $5,000 annual maximum benefit under others. Some areas that may have benefit limits include: psychiatric treatment, private-duty nursing, routine physical exams, physical therapy, convalescent-care facilities, and substance-abuse treatments.

## CAN MY COVERAGE BE CANCELED?

Will your medical coverage be canceled when you need it most, when you are sick or injured? This is one area that you *must* check out carefully before purchasing health insurance. After all, if your insurance is canceled, you may not be able to obtain a new policy. Check your policy carefully, or ask your agent what your renewal rights are. Renewal rights also pertain to the company's right to raise your premiums. The renewal provisions will say one of five things:

1. Your policy is cancelable. This means that the insurance company has the right to cancel your policy at any time, as long as it gives you written notice. It is probably not a wise decision to get this type of policy.

2. Your policy is nonrenewable. Although the company can't cancel your policy, it can refuse to renew it at the end of its term. Companies can—and often do—refuse your renewal even if you are in the middle of treatment for an illness or injury, which will make it extremely difficult for you to get another policy.

3. Your policy is conditionally renewable. This means that the company will renew your policy, except under certain conditions that they name in the policy. They can also raise your rates whenever you renew.

4. Guaranteed renewable. This means that the company will renew your policy whether you are ill or healthy. It also usually means that it can raise your rates, but only if it raises the rates for everyone who holds the same kind of policy you do. There is often a cutoff age of sixty-five when the policy is no longer guaranteed renewable.

5. Your policy is noncancelable. This means that as long as you go on paying for the policy, the company

cannot cancel it. It also means that your rates remain the same. Needless to say, this type of policy is the most expensive and is not always available.

## HOW ARE PRESCRIPTION DRUGS HANDLED UNDER MY PLAN?

There are many ways that insurance plans cover medication. Some medical plans do not cover prescription drugs at all. Others cover drugs as they would an illness; your prescription drug bills count toward your deductible and coinsurance.

Many plans cover medication as a separate expense with a separate annual deductible. For example, you may have a fifty-dollar annual deductible on prescriptions and then coverage at 100 percent.

Other policies offer the use of a prescription card. Prescription cards allow you to go into pharmacies that accept your card and pay only a nominal fee, usually a few dollars, for prescriptions. These cards range from ones that you can use at virtually any pharmacy to cards that come with a list of pharmacies that accept them.

## ARE DENTAL BILLS COVERED UNDER MY PLAN?

Most policies do not cover dental work. Sometimes dental care can be added on as a rider to your policy (for an additional cost).

## IS THERE A DEDUCTIBLE FOR MY DENTAL INSURANCE?

Dental insurance varies from company to company. While most have an annual deductible, some don't have any deductible, and others have lifetime deductibles.

Once you meet your lifetime deductible, you never have to pay a deductible again.

Most plans have different deductibles for different types of services. For instance, a plan may have no deductible for preventive services such as cleanings and checkups, and a fifty-dollar deductible for all other types of treatment.

## WHAT IS THE COINSURANCE ON MY DENTAL PROGRAM?

Dental plans usually have different levels of copayment based on the type of treatment you are receiving. Dental programs usually break treatments into four categories: Preventive care, routine care, major restorative care, and orthodontia.

A typical plan may provide 100 percent benefits for preventive care, 80 percent for routine care, and 50 percent benefits for orthodontia (braces) and restorative care.

## IS THERE A MAXIMUM AMOUNT OF BENEFITS ON MY DENTAL INSURANCE?

Many dental plans limit the amount of covered bills in any calendar year. This maximum ranges from as low as $500 to as high as $2,000. You should know what your annual maximum is so that if you've already reached this year's maximum, you can postpone work until next year when your bills will be covered again.

## HOW WOULD A TYPICAL DENTAL PLAN WORK FOR ME?

Suppose you go to the dentist for your annual checkup, which costs seventy-five dollars. Your plan has a fifty-dollar lifetime deductible and 100 percent coverage for preventive care. You would pay the fifty dollars, and then you're covered for the balance. At your checkup, your dentist, Dr. Drill, discovers three cavities and the need for two crowns. Dr. Drill fills your cavities for $300 each. Since you've already met your deductible, the fillings are covered at the routine-care rate of 80 percent. The insurance company pays $720 and you pay $180.

After the fillings, you still need two crowns. These would be covered under the restorative-care portion of the plan. Dr. Drill charges $500 a crown which would be covered at a 50-percent level, or a total of $500. Altogether the insurance company has laid out $1,245 and you have paid $730. Because you have a $1,500 annual maximum, you can receive reimbursement for further treatment if you need it.

## ARE THERE DENTAL PLANS AVAILABLE THAT ARE SIMILAR TO HMOs OR PPOs?

There are plans with sponsored dentists similar to the HMO or PPO plans. However, these plans are generally not as cost saving as the managed medical plans are, because of the existence of small coverage maximums.

## HOW CAN I KEEP COSTS DOWN ON MY HEALTH INSURANCE?

Slowing down the rising cost of health insurance has become a high priority in controlling our family budgets. If you are receiving your health insurance from work and you are only being offered one plan, there may be nothing you can do to reduce your insurance costs. However, if you are offered a choice of plans, you may consider an

HMO or PPO, or a traditional plan with a higher deductible.

If you purchase insurance on your own, good health habits, including but not limited to weight management and nonsmoking, will lower your costs. In addition, as with employer-provided policies, increasing your deductible, and adding preadmission review programs can cut costs.

## SMART HEALTH INSURANCE QUESTIONS FOR EMPLOYEES AND THE SELF-EMPLOYED

### HOW DO I PURCHASE HEALTH INSURANCE IF I AM SELF-EMPLOYED OR AM NOT COVERED AT WORK?

Everyone needs health insurance, not just those people who are fortunate enough to receive it at work. For the unemployed or self-employed, health insurance is important—and expensive. In 1988, full coverage ran from $1,200 to $3,000 a year. A less expensive route might be an HMO, but it may be difficult to find one that permits individual enrollment. You can call your state insurance department for assistance in locating one in your area.

If you are leaving a job, and if the company employs at least twenty people, you can continue coverage for up to eighteen months by paying the costs yourself. Thereafter you may be eligible to convert the group policy to an individual one, although the benefits may be reduced and the cost may be high.

### CAN I PURCHASE DENTAL INSURANCE ON MY OWN IF I AM SELF-EMPLOYED OR MY EMPLOYER DOESN'T PROVIDE IT?

Dental insurance is available on an individual basis, but it is not very cost-effective. A young man I know named Scott, who is age thirty-two and single, recently looked into purchasing dental insurance. The cost was approximately $27 a month, or $314 a year. Scott usually spends about $75 a year at the dentist. That means he would probably be reimbursed $25. So he would be spending $314 to recover $25. If his bills ran higher than expected, his maximum benefit would be only $1,000. In the end, Scott decided it was foolish to spend $314 for a potential maximum benefit of $1,000.

## DOES MY EMPLOYER PROVIDE HEALTH INSURANCE?

Most mid- to large-size companies in our country offer their employees medical insurance. Sometimes the company pays the entire cost of your coverage; sometimes you might be asked to share the costs. Health insurance can be one of the best perks of any job, and it can be a strong consideration when you are thinking about leaving your present job or taking a new one.

## WHOM DO I SPEAK TO AT WORK ABOUT HEALTH INSUR-ANCE?

Knowing the right people to speak to can greatly simplify your life. This is a great question to ask your immediate supervisor or manager. You might also check with the personnel department, the comptroller, the human-resources department, the employee-benefits department, the shop steward, the office manager, or possibly the insurance company itself.

Many employers offer you a choice of medical-insurance programs with vastly different features so you can pick out the one which serves your needs the best. A client of mine in the electronics manufacturing business offers his employees a choice of six different plans—

which provides many benefits to his employees, but can also get very confusing. Even if your employer offers only one program, health-insurance policies can be confusing, with deductibles, coinsurance, coverage maximums, and limitations. If you do have insurance at work, you'll probably be issued a benefits booklet, or employee handbook, which will explain simple procedures and concepts in the most confusing manner possible. The insurance expert at your job is an important person to befriend so that this benefit book can be translated back into English.

## ARE THERE ANY REASONS WHY I, OR ANY OF MY DEPENDENTS, COULD LOSE THE MEDICAL INSURANCE I HAVE AT WORK?

There are many reasons (called qualifying events) why you may lose coverage at work:
- You may quit or get laid off.
- Your employer may choose not to provide benefits anymore.
- Your children may get too old to be covered under the plan.
- Your family's coverage may end if you get divorced or die.

## IF ANY OF THE ABOVE EVENTS HAPPENS, WHEN DOES MY COVERAGE ACTUALLY END?

Generally your insurance will stop on the day the qualifying event occurs. However, many companies have policies that continue an employee's insurance until the end of the month in which they leave the company. You should know whether or not your company has such a policy, particularly if you are contemplating leaving and want to time the move to your maximum advantage. If your employer will continue health insurance until the end of the month, it is a better idea to leave the first week of a month rather than the last week of the previous month. That way you get three or four weeks of "free" coverage.

## IF MY HEALTH INSURANCE ENDS, CAN I CONTINUE THE COVERAGE MYSELF?

If the company you work for has over twenty employees and is not a government agency or a church, you can elect to continue your insurance at your own cost. This is done through a federal law called the Congressional Omnibus Budget Reconciliation Act, or COBRA.

Many health-insurance plans have conversion features that allow you to convert to an individual major-medical insurance policy at the end of your coverage under the group plan. These conversion plans vary widely from insurer to insurer. Most conversion plans offer very poor coverage and should only be accepted if medical coverage can't be obtained elsewhere. A typical plan will have a $500 deductible and a maximum lifetime benefit of $50,000. Most Blue Cross/Blue Shield programs offer conversion plans that are comparable to the terminated group plan.

COBRA has allowed many people to bridge the gap in medical coverage while in between jobs or waiting to be picked up by a new employer's health-insurance plan. Understanding the benefits you can receive under this law can greatly enhance your ability to make maximum use of it. Asking the right questions of your COBRA administrator at work can decrease the likelihood that you will fall between the cracks if you or anyone in your family loses medical coverage at work.

## WHAT RATES WILL I BE CHARGED IF I ELECT TO CONTINUE MY COVERAGE UNDER COBRA?

Your employer cannot charge you any more than the group rate for the plan, plus 2 percent. The 2 percent is for administrative charges incurred to comply with COBRA. However, your COBRA rate is not necessarily better than a rate for a plan you obtain on your own.

## HOW CAN COBRA GROUP RATES BE HIGHER THAN COMPARABLE INDIVIDUAL RATES?

Group rates are often based on an average age of all employees at a company. If your company has a lot of older employees, and you are in a younger age bracket, you may be able to purchase health insurance for less money than the company's group rates.

## CAN I CONTINUE MY COVERAGE UNDER COBRA INDEFINITELY?

As an ex-employee, you can continue your health insurance under your former employer's group plan for up to eighteen months—as long as the plan is still in effect for remaining employees, and as long as you do not get coverage under another group plan.

## CAN MY DEPENDENTS CONTINUE THEIR HEALTH INSURANCE?

Usually, members of your family are covered as dependents under your group medical plan. There may come a time when their coverage is terminated because they no longer qualify as dependents. In such a case they can continue their coverage for up to thirty-six months. For example, a child who has been covered under your plan while in college may lose his insurance upon graduation. However, he may desire to exercise his COBRA rights while undertaking a job hunt.

There are several occasions that may be considered a qualifying event (a reason for losing coverage) for a dependent:

- Death of a covered employee
- Divorce or legal separation of an employee and spouse
- An employee becoming eligible for Medicare
- A child becoming too old to be covered as a child

## IS MY CONTINUATION OF COVERAGE AUTOMATIC, OR MUST I REQUEST IT?

Medical coverage is not ordinarily continued automatically and must be requested in writing. A potential COBRA beneficiary has sixty days from his qualifying event to elect coverage. Once a person has elected continuation of health insurance, it is his responsibility to pay the premium each month to the employer or risk being dropped from coverage.

## WHOM DO I SEE AT WORK ABOUT ELECTING COBRA?

Generally, the person who runs the medical plan is the one to talk to about COBRA. You should receive written notification at least twice from this person: initially when you enroll in a plan and then again when a qualifying event occurs. It is a good idea to find out the name of the person in charge of COBRA continuation even if you don't think you'll need it, because employers are not always well versed in COBRA administration.

## SMART HEALTH INSURANCE QUESTIONS FOR EMPLOYERS

### I OWN A MIDSIZE COMPANY. WHICH IS BETTER FOR MY COMPANY, A BASIC PLAN OR A MAJOR-MEDICAL PLAN?

Many small and midsize companies today are finding that medical insurance is becoming their largest employee-related expense next to wages. Basic coverage used to be enough to cover the bulk of employees' medical bills. However, with modern medical procedures and skyrocketing medical costs, it isn't quite enough anymore.

Many companies actually "piggyback" the two types of plans to provide the maximum coverage at the best possible price. The basic plan may provide hospitalization while the major medical covers medical bills after a deductible is paid. This is called a wraparound plan.

Another popular alternative is having a basic hospitalization plan and a basic medical plan supplemented by a major-medical plan for larger medical bills. This is called a supplemental plan.

### HOW DO I CHOOSE BETWEEN A WRAPAROUND, SUPPLEMENTAL, OR COMPREHENSIVE MEDICAL PLAN FOR OUR EMPLOYEES?

There are many opinions on this question with no clear-cut answer. Most quality health-insurance programs offer similar benefits. The differences are often minor despite the large emphasis placed on them by the competing companies.

Most benefits managers today decide on the type of medical plan for their company based on the best value. Comprehensive plans (one plan under which both hospitalization and major medical are covered) are very often the best value for companies with young employees, while wraparound and supplemental programs are often the best alternatives for companies with older employees.

## WHAT EXACTLY IS BLUE CROSS AND BLUE SHIELD AND SHOULD IT BE PART OF MY COMPANY'S MEDICAL PROGRAM?

Blue Cross and Blue Shield, collectively known as "the blues," are really many companies, mostly nonprofit, which provide health-care insurance. Each state has its own Blue Cross/Blue Shield association; some states (such as New York) have several.

The blues historically have been the biggest providers of basic medical-insurance programs. Blue Cross provides the basic hospitalization and Blue Shield provides the basic surgical and physician expenses. In recent years the blues have begun to offer major-medical insurance, which was previously the domain of the private insurance carrier. Their programs are similar to the ones that private carriers are offering. The blues are more tightly regulated by state governments, which has resulted in a lack of flexibility in their programs. The tight regulation has not, however, resulted in better benefits or lower cost.

## ARE THERE ANY ADVANTAGES OF A MANAGED CARE PLAN FOR MY COMPANY?

Participants in managed care plans (such as HMOs and PPOs) are offered the opportunity to receive high-quality health care without the payment of large deductible or copayments as long as they use a physician sponsored by the plan. Employers benefit because the premiums on these plans are usually substantially less than those for comparable traditional medical plans.

About four years ago, a local medical laboratory decided to offer a PPO plan in an attempt to lower soaring costs. No one, including the insurance agent, really expected the employees to be interested in participating in the plan. They were all wrong. The employees accepted the plan enthusiastically, and each year more and more of the lab's employees migrate into that medical option.

## HOW DO I CHOOSE A MANAGED CARE PROGRAM FOR MY COMPANY?

There are many factors an employer should look at when choosing a managed care program, the most important of these being quantity and quality of doctors.

Another important consideration is cost. Managed care programs should usually be cost-saving measures. If the cost of the plan is more expensive than comparable traditional plans, something is wrong.

## IS A FREEDOM PLAN AVAILABLE FOR MY COMPANY AND DOES IT MAKE SENSE?

Freedom plans offer employees the benefit of a choice between a traditional plan and a managed care plan with the same insurance company, with the ability to switch back and forth between them. A person might choose to use the PPO for routine physicals, but use his own specialist and pay a deductible for any major problems.

Very often older employees with established doctor relationships will opt for the traditional plan, while younger employees without physicians will choose to use the doctors from the plan.

## CAN I OFFER A MANAGED CARE PLAN FOR THOSE WHO WANT IT WITHOUT GETTING A FREEDOM PLAN AND CHANGING MY EXISTING COVERAGE?

Yes. In fact, if your company has more than twenty-five employees and your company has received a request from a qualified HMO in a geographic area where at least twenty-five employees reside, you must offer an HMO on the same basis that you are offering your health insurance now. This is called a dual-choice option and has resulted in many employees subscribing to HMOs.

## MUST MY COMPANY CONTRIBUTE TO THE COST OF THE HMO?

The federal HMO law requires you to contribute to the HMO on the same basis that you are contributing to the traditional major-medical plan if mandated under the dual-choice plan. However, you are not required to contribute more than the premium. For instance, if XYZ Inc. is contributing $200 per month per employee for insurance, but an HMO only costs $120 per month, the employee is not entitled to the $80 difference. XYZ Inc. is only required to contribute the cost of the HMO.

# DISABILITY INSURANCE

## THE BASICS

## WHAT IS DISABILITY INSURANCE?

Disability insurance pays you an income when you are sick or hurt and can't work—it steps in and replaces the "money-making machine" when it breaks down.

## HOW CAN I GET DISABILITY INSURANCE?

Disability insurance may be provided at work or purchased directly through your insurance agent (the same agent from whom you purchase your health insurance).

## ARE THERE DIFFERENT TYPES OF DISABILITY INSURANCE?

Disability insurance comes in several forms:

***Long-term disability income insurance***: Long-term disability income insurance will pay you a monthly benefit for a benefit period specified in your policy, or for the duration of the disability, whichever is shorter.

***Short-term disability income insurance***: Short-term disability income insurance is provided by a company to its employees to pay a percentage of salary for a short amount of time, usually up to six months. Several states require by law that this benefit is provided to all employees.

***Business-overhead-expense insurance***: Business-overhead-expense insurance is disability insurance that steps in and pays the business expenses of a business owner while he is disabled.

***Disability buy-out insurance***: Business buyout insurance provides money to enable one partner to buy out another in the event one becomes disabled.

All of the types of disability insurance serve specific purposes and situations; some people may benefit from a combination of types. A doctor is a good example of someone who may need a disability combination: long- and short-term income insurance to replace his income if he should become disabled, business-overhead insurance to pay the expenses of his practice while he is disabled, and buyout insurance to enable his partners to buy his interest in the business if he is unable to return to work.

## HOW DOES DISABILITY INSURANCE WORK?

It works when you can't. Disability, or income-replace-ment, insurance provides you with money after you have been out of work for a specified period of time, called the elimination period.

The income will be paid to you for another specified period of time, called the benefit period, or until you return to work—whichever is shorter. Generally, the shorter the elimination period and the longer the benefit period, the more expensive the policy.

## WHAT IS THE DEFINITION OF DISABILITY IN MY POLICY?

Rarely is the requirement for collecting benefits as sim-ple as being out of work due to medical problems. You must understand how disability is defined in your policy in order to understand under what conditions you will or will not qualify for benefits.

The best policies have an "own occupation" definition of disability. This means that you can collect benefits if you can't perform the material and substantial duties of your old job, even if you are able to work in another occupation.

Suppose you are a computer programmer whose arthritis is so severe that you can no longer operate a computer. You would collect benefits even if you are teaching English at a nearby college.

Disability may also be defined as the inability to per-form the material and substantial duties of the occupa-tion for which you have been trained and skilled. You may be recovered from your illness, for example, but not able to return to your former occupation. If a corporate executive suffers a heart attack, the doctors may advise him to stop working because he can't handle the stress of his business. He should not be expected to get a job as a basket weaver, which is below his educational and income standards, and should be able to collect disability benefits because of his inability to handle the stress involved in his business.

Disability may be defined as the inability to perform *any* occupation for which you are trained and skilled. The computer operator now teaching English would not be able to collect benefits under this definition, because he is able to earn a living, even though it's not through his original occupation.

## WON'T SOCIAL SECURITY PAY ME A BENEFIT IF I AM DIS-ABLED?

The sad truth is that very few people ever collect any money from Social Security for a disability. The requirements to collect are so stringent that it is nearly impossible to collect any benefits while still alive.

Social Security requires that an applicant for benefits be so severely impaired that he cannot perform any gainful work. The disability must be expected to last twelve months or to result in premature death. Furthermore, the maximum benefit a person would be eligible to receive is extremely small when compared with what you might receive through private insurance, and would probably not be enough to provide for a comfortable existence.

## HOW MUCH DISABILITY-INCOME INSURANCE DO I NEED?

The rule of thumb is to secure enough insurance to cover your after-tax living expenses. Most insurance companies limit the policyholder to approximately 60 percent of his gross income. Most states limit the amount of disability you can purchase, based on your income. If you make $100,000 a year, for example, you cannot purchase a $200,000 disability policy. These laws are put into effect to give you the incentive to go back to work.

Many insurance agents will tell you to acquire as much disability insurance as you are allowed by law. However, it's important to remember that disability insurance is designed to provide you with an income when you can't, not to make you rich.

To find out how much disability you need, you must first determine how much money you currently earn per month, and how much you currently spend. Then find out how much disability you would receive from Social Security, and how much from any current policies you might have at work or any other sources. That should help you determine if you need to purchase any more insurance to cover your expenses.

## IF I AM DISABLED, WHEN WILL I START RECEIVING BENEFITS?

All disability policies stipulate that you must wait a certain amount of time, called the elimination period, before you start collecting benefits. Elimination periods range anywhere from 15 to 365 days.

The length of the waiting period is one of the factors that determines how much your policy will cost. The longer the elimination period, the less your premiums. If you choose a long waiting period, be sure that you have enough savings to be able to survive for that period of time without receiving any income.

If you want a short elimination period but can't afford it, one solution may be to purchase a combination of policies with different waiting periods. For example, you may purchase a policy with a short waiting period to cover only the amount of your mortgage, and purchase a second policy with a longer elimination period for the balance of your needs.

## HOW LONG WILL I BE PAID IF I AM SICK AND CAN'T WORK?

This is the second factor that will determine how much you spend on premiums. The "benefits period" differs from policy to policy. Short-term insurance may cover anywhere from six months to two years. Long-term insurance may go on for much longer. This is a very important question to ask, so that you can make provisions for other sources of income if necessary.

## HOW WILL I RECEIVE MY BENEFIT PAYMENTS?

This differs from policy to policy. Some will pay you by the month, and some will send you weekly checks. In certain cases you may receive a lump-sum payment.

## ARE THERE ANY RESTRICTIONS ON MY POLICY?

There are two standard restrictions that are found in most policies. They are:

- Injury due to an act of war
- Injury caused by committing a felony

Other restrictions to look out for: Does the disability policy you are purchasing cover all other causes, or are specific diseases, such as AIDS, not covered? Read the policy carefully, or ask your agent to list all diseases not covered under the policy. Are preexisting conditions covered? Suppose you have a bad knee when you purchase the policy. Your policy may include a rider that claims that any disabilities due to an injury to that knee will not be covered.

Other typical restrictions include disabilities resulting from drug abuse, attempted suicide, and crashes of non-commercial airplanes.

## IS PREGNANCY COVERED UNDER MY POLICY?

Most policies do not cover normal pregnancies. They may, however, cover disabilities caused by complications in pregnancy. Disability policies covering pregnancy are not maternity-leave policies; they only cover you for as long as the pregnancy or complications inhibit your ability to work and earn a living.

## IF I AM DISABLED BUT ONLY SUFFER A PARTIAL LOSS OF INCOME, CAN I STILL COLLECT BENEFITS?

Two popular options on disability policies are "partial benefit" and "residual benefit" provisions.

Partial benefits are paid if you suffer a partial loss of income without ever being fully disabled. Residual benefits are paid if you continue to have a partial loss of income after a period of total disability. If you have the potential to suffer a partial loss of income, both of these options are probably good ideas.

If you choose these options, make sure that a partial disability can satisfy your elimination period or you may find yourself with fewer benefits than you expected. Many policies require you to be fully disabled and not able to work during the elimination period in order to collect partial benefits.

## IS THERE ANY WAY I COULD COLLECT THE TOTAL DISABILITY BENEFIT, EVEN IF I'M ABLE TO WORK?

There is a provision called "presumptive total disability" that will allow your policy to pay your total benefit if you meet certain conditions, even if you can work. A typical presumptive total disability benefit will go into effect if you lose your sight, hearing, or use of two limbs. Although it may at first seem that any of the above conditions would be truly disabling, many people can and do return to work after such traumas.

A computer consultant I know suffers from multiple sclerosis and still runs his own business, despite the fact that he has lost use of his legs. Since he bought a policy with presumptive total disability before he got sick, he is now collecting benefits while working full-time.

## CAN I RENEW MY POLICY AS LONG AS I KEEP WORKING?

If you should choose to keep working past age sixty-five, will your policy keep working with you? A client of mine had an old disability policy he had purchased twenty years ago. The policy was only renewable until he was fifty-five. This old policy was outdated and did not suit his needs; unfortunately, his current health situation prevented him from purchasing a replacement. The best policies available today are renewable as long as you keep working, even for life. However, even policies that previously had lifetime benefit periods will usually pay benefits for only two years after you reach the age of sixty-five.

FINANCES AND DISABILITY

## IF I BECOME DISABLED, DO I STILL HAVE TO PAY PREMIUMS?

This is a good question to ask when purchasing your policy, because all policies are different. If you are receiving disability benefits and living on a reduced income, it could become difficult to make the premium payments. Some policies allow you to stop making payments when you're collecting disability, and others do not. Since those that do usually do not charge extra for it, it is to your benefit to seek out this type of policy.

## IS THE BENEFIT I RECEIVE FROM DISABILITY INSURANCE TAXABLE?

If you pay for the policy with money that you have paid taxes on, the benefits will come to you income-tax free. If the policy is a group policy and your employer pays the premium, the benefits will be taxable. It is obviously more desirable whenever possible to receive the disability benefits on a tax-free basis. Many people who have group disability policies at work, which would make the benefits taxable, buy small individual policies. That way, if they become disabled they can use the money received from their individual policy to pay the tax on money received from the group benefits.

## HOW CAN I MAKE SURE THAT MY DISABILITY POLICY KEEPS UP WITH THE PACE OF INFLATION?

A policy that covers your income needs today may be too small five years from now. If you remain healthy, an annual review and purchase of new insurance as needed will keep the policy concurrent with rising costs.

However, if you become disabled and are receiving benefits, it may not be possible to purchase new insurance despite the fact that your income needs increase. Most insurance companies offer two solutions to this problem: a guaranteed insurability rider and a cost-of-living rider.

## WHAT IS A GUARANTEED INSURABILITY RIDER?

A guaranteed insurability rider, also known as a purchase option rider, is an optional benefit that allows you to purchase additional insurance without having to prove that you are still in good health. Typically, a policy will allow you to purchase additional benefits each year on the policy anniversary if you qualify financially. In fact, many policies even allow you to make one purchase while you are receiving benefits. This rider makes it very convenient to keep your disability program up to date because it is very easy to increase your coverage.

## WHAT IS A COST-OF-LIVING BENEFIT?

A cost-of-living benefit, also known as COLA, is an optional rider you can purchase that increases the amount of benefit payable during a period of disability. The benefits increase based on a flat schedule such as 4 or 7 percent, or based on adjustments to the Consumer Price Index. For example, if you are receiving $1,000 a month in disability, your benefits will be increased by $40 each year if you continue to be disabled and have a 4-percent COLA.

## SHOULD I TAKE A COLA BENEFIT OR A PURCHASE OPTION?

Each rider has its place and it may be a good idea to purchase both of them. The purchase option will help ensure that your policy keeps up with your needs. The COLA will protect you from inflation eating away at your purchasing power, if you become disabled for a substantial period of time.

If you had a $3,000/month policy with three $500 purchase options and a 7-percent COLA, the policy would work in the following manner: At the first, second, and third anniversaries, you could exercise your options and purchase additional insurance. The policy would then grow in size to $4,500 a month. If in the fourth year, you become disabled, your policy would pay you $4,500 a month. Every year you remain disabled, the COLA would increase the benefit by 7 percent. Therefore, if you were still disabled in the fifth year, your benefit would grow by $315 to $4,814 per month, thus reducing or even negating the effects of inflation.

## ARE THERE ANY OTHER WAYS TO INCREASE MY BENEFIT EACH YEAR?

Many policies have an automatic increase in benefits built into them. Each year on the anniversary the policy increases by some percentage, usually around 5 percent. However, the automatic increase also includes an automatic increase in premium. A $1,000/month disability policy purchased a year ago would pay benefits of $1,050 this year if it had an automatic increase included. The premium for this policy would increase by slightly more than 5 percent, say from $300 annually to $318 annually, because you would be a year older.

## Association Policies

### I BELONG TO A PROFESSIONAL ASSOCIATION. CAN I PURCHASE DISABILITY INSURANCE THROUGH IT?

Many work-related organizations and professional associations offer disability insurance to their members at substantial discounts. Association policies are made available to any member in good standing in the organization. The type of policy your association offers may vary widely in quality from another association or from what is available privately.

## ARE THERE DIFFERENT TYPES OF ASSOCIATION POLICIES?

Association policies come in two basic forms: individual policies with a volume discount, and group policies.

Individual policies bought through an association offer all the benefits of high-quality noncancelable individual policies with a discount given to the purchaser for being a member of the sponsoring association.

Group association policies are sold to the association and each member can enroll on the policy. Group policies are generally less expensive than individual policies.

## ARE THERE ANY DISADVANTAGES TO ASSOCIATION POLICIES?

Association policies usually provide a substantial savings over a comparable policy purchased individually. It is important for you to evaluate an association policy, make sure it fits your needs and that you're not buying it just because it's less expensive.

For example, a policy that is not guaranteed renewable might not be appropriate for a young person with a mortgage and a growing family. An attorney I know was shocked to find out the policy he was considering had a substantial cutback in the size of his policy at age fifty-five when he would still have a child in college and an active practice. Many of these association policies are very rigid and may not fit your needs at all—so be sure to question your agent or association representative.

## WHAT HAPPENS IF I'M NO LONGER A MEMBER OF THIS ASSOCIATION?

Many association policies require continued membership in the association to continue the policy. If you purchase a policy from your association and drop your membership, are you also dropping your policy? Be sure you ask this question before you purchase the insurance. Don't wait until you're ready to leave the organization.

## IF I DO LEAVE THE ASSOCIATION, OR IF THE ASSOCIATION DOES NOT OFFER THAT DISABILITY POLICY ANY LONGER, CAN I PICK UP THE POLICY AND PAY FOR IT DIRECTLY?

If you leave the association and your health deteriorates, it may not be possible to acquire other disability insurance. This became a very important consideration for a young pharmacist in New York who purchased disability insurance through his professional association. Last year he came down with cancer and subsequently left the association. Because his policy had a "pickup" option (allowing him to maintain the policy), he is now receiving disability payments while undergoing treatment—even though he is no longer a member of the pharmacists' association.

## CAN I OBTAIN LONG-TERM DISABILITY INSURANCE AT WORK?

Many companies provide their employees with disability insurance as part of the benefits package. Many of those who do not offer disability insurance as part of their employee benefits, do allow their employees to purchase disability insurance by taking the premiums directly from their salary. Ask your employer if this is an option available to you.

## DISABILITY FOR MY BUSINESS

### SHOULD I PURCHASE ANY DISABILITY POLICIES TO PROTECT MY BUSINESS?

What would happen to your company or business if you were not able to work for a sizable period? Disabilities to a key executive and/or owner of a small company can put severe strains on the ability of that business to make money.

There are policies called business-overhead-expense policies that will step in and pay the expenses of a business if the owner should become disabled and can't work. These policies will usually pay benefits for only a short period of time. The intention of the policy is to keep the business going until the owner can come back to work or sell the business. The biggest purchasers of these policies are professionals and business owners who actively participate in the day-to-day activities of the business, such as doctors in private practice, plumbers, electricians, etc.

### IS THERE A POLICY FOR A BUSINESS BUYOUT AGREEMENT?

Small businesses may face a problem if one of the owners becomes disabled and can't hold up his or her end of the responsibilities. Business buyout policies will pay a benefit either in a lump sum or over time to fund these agreements.

A dry-cleaning business in my neighborhood has an arrangement that calls for a buyout in the event of death or disability of either of its partners. The purchase price is preset at $250,000 for each partner's interest. In the event of death, a life-insurance policy pays its death benefit immediately. If either should become disabled, an overhead expense policy pays benefits for two years and then a disability buyout policy pays a lump sum to fund the agreement. The existence of these policies and corresponding insurance helps keep the business whole in the event of a catastrophe.

# SENIOR-CARE INSURANCE

## MEDICARE

### WHAT IS MEDICARE?

Health-care costs have been rising at astronomical rates for several years. Nowhere is this increase in costs more apparent than in care for the elderly. Modern medical techniques are helping us to live longer, fuller lives at a tremendous cost. The portion of the United States' population that is over sixty-five is growing at about 2 percent a year. Furthermore, the portion of that group that is over age seventy-five is also increasing at a very steady rate. The aging of our population has created a need for very special insurance products to take care of the special needs of the elderly.

The government has tried to address these issues through Medicare. Medicare is the federal health-insurance program for people age sixty-five or older. Certain disabled people may also qualify for Medicare. You don't have to be eligible for Social Security to be eligible for Medicare, and you can still be working and receive Medicare benefits. Medicare is divided into two parts: Part A (hospital insurance) and Part B (medical insurance).

## HOW DO I SIGN UP FOR MEDICARE?

If you or your spouse are eligible for Social Security benefits, enrollment in Part A coverage is automatic when you reach age sixty-five. If you have not paid into the Social Security system, you can purchase Part A coverage. The monthly premium for Part A, if your coverage is not automatic, was $177/month in 1991.

Medicare Part B is optional and is offered to all Medicare participants when they enroll in Part A. Part B can be obtained whether or not your Part-A coverage is automatic or purchased. The monthly premium for Part B in 1991 was $29.90. The Part-B premium is usually deducted from your monthly Social Security checks. If you enroll for initial coverage in either part, after age sixty-five your premium will be greater. You can get information about enrolling for Medicare at your local Social Security office.

## WHAT DOES PART A COVER?

Medicare Part A covers the hospitalization part of your health insurance. Coverage includes items such as semiprivate room and board and miscellaneous hospital supplies. Diagnostic tests, nursing care, special diets, and physical therapy may be included as part of the services and supplies. Home health care, skilled nursing facilities, and hospice care would also be covered under Part A. The rule of thumb is: If it is not treatment by a physician, it is probably covered under Part A.

## ARE ALL BENEFITS UNDER PART A COVERED IN FULL?

Part-A benefits are subject to a time limit and a dollar deductible. The hospital coverage is based on a benefit period, which starts on the day you enter the hospital and ends when you have been out of the hospital for sixty days in a row. The number of benefit periods you use is unlimited. In addition, Part A has a deductible for each benefit period of $628. Benefit periods are covered in the following manner:

- You are responsible for the first $628.
- After the deductible, the first sixty days are covered in full.
- From days sixty-one to ninety, you pay the first $157 a day and Medicare pays the balance.
- After ninety days, your benefits end unless you have any lifetime reserve days. If you do, you pay the first $314 and Medicare pays the balance until your reserve days are used up.

Everyone receives sixty lifetime reserve days to use for hospital care when needed. You can use them all at once, if necessary, or save days for later use.

## DO ALL HOSPITALS ACCEPT MEDICARE?

Most hospitals accept Medicare and will bill Medicare directly. After the bill is processed, you will get an explanation from Medicare showing the portion you still have to pay in deductibles or coinsurances.

## DO THE DAYS I SPEND IN A SKILLED-NURSING FACILITY COUNT TOWARD MY BENEFIT PERIODS UNDER THE HOSPITAL PART OF PART A?

Yes. However, the payment schedule is different. The first twenty days spent in a skilled-nursing facility during a benefit period are covered in full. From the twenty-first through the one-hundredth day, Medicare pays for all but $78.50 a day. After one hundred days in each benefit period, you are on your own; Medicare does not provide coverage.

## DO ALL NURSING HOMES ACCEPT MEDICARE?

Most nursing homes are not certified by Medicare as skilled-nursing facilities and are not eligible for reimbursement by Medicare. It is important to find out in advance whether or not your facility participates in Medicare so that you are not faced with unexpected expenses.

## ARE THERE ANY SIGNIFICANT RESTRICTIONS ON THE COVERAGE PROVIDED FOR SKILLED-NURSING FACILITIES?

There are many restrictions associated with Medicare. The primary one is that Medicare will only cover treatment at a facility designed to help you recover from an illness or an injury. It will not cover custodial nursing care for people who need help with daily living activities such as eating, bathing, dressing, and walking. Coverage under Medicare is intended to be temporary and to treat only specific conditions.

## ARE THERE ANY OTHER RESTRICTIONS ASSOCIATED WITH SKILLED-NURSING FACILITIES?

The main factor in determining benefits is whether or not the treatment is medically necessary. In order to ensure that it is a necessary medical treatment, Medicare also requires that you enter the facility within thirty days of leaving the hospital. Furthermore, a doctor must prescribe the nursing facility as treatment for an ongoing condition for which you were hospitalized.

## ARE ANY HOME-HEALTH-CARE EXPENSES COVERED UNDER PART A?

Like nursing-home coverage, home health care is covered when the services are medically necessary. Home health care, including physical, occupational and speech therapy, nursing care, and medical supplies and equipment may be covered under both Parts A and B; the services will always be paid for by Part-A coverage when you are eligible under both parts.

## ARE THERE ANY DEDUCTIBLES ASSOCIATED WITH HOME HEALTH CARE?

There are no deductibles associated with the Medicare coverage of home health care as long as certain conditions are met:

- The services are prescribed as part of a home-health-care plan set up by your doctor.
- Care is provided by a home-health-care plan set up by your doctor.
- Services include intermittent, part-time skilled-nursing care, physical therapy, or speech therapy.
- You are confined to your home.

## WHAT HOME HEALTH SERVICES ARE NOT COVERED BY MEDICARE?

Many times when elderly people are sick or injured, they have problems taking care of their everyday needs, such as cooking and cleaning. Unfortunately, these homemaker services, as well as full-time skilled-nursing care, while often necessary, are not covered by Medicare.

## WHAT OTHER SERVICES ARE COVERED UNDER PART A OF MEDICARE?

Coverage is also provided for care in a Medicare-certified hospice for terminally ill patients.

## WHAT DOES PART B COVER?

Part B is the medical and surgical portion of Medicare and will cover the charges associated with a person providing a service. Typical charges covered by Part B include physician charges, emergency-room services, X rays, physical therapy, and blood and diagnostic tests, including mammographies and pap smears.

## IS THERE A DEDUCTIBLE FOR MEDICARE PART B?

Part B has a very simple deductible of $100 per year. This means that each year, before you can collect any money from Medicare, you must pay $100 out-of-pocket. In addition, there is a blood deductible: you must pay for the first three pints of blood you use in a year before Medicare picks up the cost.

## IS THERE ANY OTHER MONEY THAT I MIGHT HAVE TO LAY OUT?

After you pay the deductible, you are responsible for 20 percent of Medicare's reasonable charges. Reasonable charges are the approved amount that Medicare will reimburse. Medicare-approved charges are based on customary rates for the same procedure in your area. Health-care providers can charge more than Medicare's approved charges, and in that case you would be responsible for the difference.

## ARE THERE ANY LIMITATIONS TO WHAT A DOCTOR CAN CHARGE?

Many states have limits on how much more than reasonable charges a provider can bill his Medicare patients for Medicare-covered procedures. For example, a state law may limit a doctor to charge no more than 115 percent of the Medicare-approved rate for a particular procedure. Federal law limits a doctor's charge for routine home and office visits to 140 percent of the approved Medicare amount.

## IS THERE ANY WAY THAT I CAN ENSURE MY DOCTOR DOESN'T BILL MORE THAN THE MEDICARE-ALLOWABLE AMOUNT?

Medicare has a program whereby physicians and other medical providers agree to accept Medicare's reasonable charge as full payment for all Medicare patients. If you choose a doctor from this program, you will only have to pay the yearly $100 deductible and 20 percent of the bill. These providers are all available on a list you can get from your local Medicare office.

Many physicians will accept the Medicare-allowable amount even if they are not part of the participating provider's program. If you are a Medicare patient, you should check with your doctor and find out if she will accept Medicare's reasonable charge.

## WHERE CAN I FIND OUT MORE ABOUT MEDICARE?

Information can be obtained from a Medicare handbook, which you receive when you enroll in the program. If you need more information, you can write or call your local Medicare office. Rules vary slightly from state to state, so it is important to check the rules where you live.

## MEDICARE SUPPLEMENTAL INSURANCE

### DO I NEED MEDICAL INSURANCE IN ADDITION TO MEDICARE?

Anyone who has ever had a medical claim under Medicare knows that there are many weaknesses in its coverage. Twenty percent of a large medical bill can be a lot of money. In addition, doctors often charge more than Medicare considers reasonable. If you are a senior citizen, it's probably a good idea to carry additional insurance.

### WHAT KIND OF EXTRA INSURANCE SHOULD I CARRY?

Many senior citizens make the same mistake as did Sam, an old friend of my family. Sam had recently retired. For the first time in his life, he had to purchase medical insurance for his wife and himself, having been covered previously by various employers. Sam and his wife were covered by Medicare A and B, but purchased a major-medical policy to be sure they had enough coverage. Unfortunately, Sam didn't ask the right questions and ended up paying for a policy that duplicated his Medicare coverage and didn't fill in the holes left by it. He could have saved himself a lot of money by purchasing "Medicare supplemental insurance," which covers only what Medicare doesn't.

### WHERE WOULD I OBTAIN MEDICARE SUPPLEMENTAL INSURANCE?

The first place to look for health coverage is from your former employer or union. Many companies, particularly those with union employees, provide health insurance to their retirees.

The second place to look is your insurance agent, or regional Blue Cross/Blue Shield office. Many state insurance commissioners publish a book outlining the policies offered in their state. Good insurance agents and brokers will have this booklet at their disposal to show you the features of the different policies available.

## WHAT DO MEDICARE SUPPLEMENTAL POLICIES COVER?

Supplemental policies come in two basic forms. The first type covers the deductible and the 20-percent coinsurance amount on Medicare's reasonable charges. If your doctor charges more than Medicare allows and you have one of these policies, you still have to pay the difference yourself.

The second type of policy is more comprehensive, and more expensive. It covers, within certain limits, what Medicare doesn't. This type of policy is not appropriate for everyone, especially if your physician is part of a participating-provider organization as mentioned earlier, or is part of an HMO.

## WHAT FEATURES SHOULD I LOOK FOR IN A MEDICARE SUPPLEMENT POLICY?

The most basic features of any Medicare supplement policy should include coverage for the hospital deductibles under Medicare Part A and the 20-percent coinsurance amount after the $100 deductible under Part B. The other feature that should always be included is coverage for the first three pints of blood each year for which Medicare does not pay. Many states require that a policy must cover the three points just listed in order to qualify as a Medicare supplement policy.

There are many other features and coverages that policies may provide, including: private-duty nursing, prescription drugs, charges in excess of Medicare's reasonable charges, and medical care received in a foreign country.

## IS THIS POLICY GUARANTEED RENEWABLE?

As with other kinds of health insurance, it is very important to make sure you are purchasing a policy that can't be terminated. Renewability is also related to the track record of the company issuing the insurance. Today's economic climate warrants taking a very strong look at how long a company has been in the senior-care market, and how committed they are to staying in it. Many companies in the health-insurance field have recently stopped issuing senior-care insurance due to declining profits. If you have medical problems, it may be difficult to get new insurance, so be sure you are signing on with an established, reputable company.

## ARE THERE ANY EXCLUSIONS OR LIMITATIONS ON THIS POLICY?

This is a very important question for you to ask, because you don't want to have ongoing health problems that are not covered. Very often policies will exclude such specific illnesses as Alzheimer's disease or schizophrenia. Make sure your policy does not.

\* \* \*

## ARE THERE ANY DOLLAR MAXIMUMS ON THE BENEFITS I CAN RECEIVE UNDER THIS POLICY?

Does your Medicare supplement policy have a maximum lifetime or annual benefit? Geriatric care has improved tremendously in recent years, and senior citizens are living longer after illnesses that once would have killed them. Longer lives, however, mean more medical treatment and more bills. So you must be sure that your policy provides you with adequate coverage throughout your life.

## LONG-TERM CARE

## WHAT IS LONG-TERM CARE?

Long-term care is health care you receive if you are incapacitated from illness or injury and cannot care for yourself. Long-term care may include aid in meeting the daily necessities for life (such as eating and bathing), nursing care, and medical care. These services may be received in a nursing home or in your house. For instance, a stroke victim will often require long-term care while relearning to function normally.

## WHY DO I NEED LONG-TERM-CARE INSURANCE?

Many of us have suffered through seeing a relative's health deteriorate to the point where it was impossible to take care of her or him without professional help, either at home or in a nursing home. One of the biggest problems in health care today is the long-term health needs of the nation's elderly. A friend of mine recently had to put his mother, who was suffering from Alzheimer's disease, in a nursing home. He estimated the annual cost for the home to be $45,000!

Many people, my friend included, believe that health insurance and Medicare will pay these bills. Unfortunately, the sad truth is that very few health-insurance policies cover long-term custodial and maintenance care for an incapacitated person.

## WHAT HAPPENS IF I SHOULD HAVE TO ENTER A NURSING HOME?

Traditionally, nursing-home expenses have been borne by the family of the nursing-home resident, often utilizing the assets of the resident until these assets were exhausted. Once the assets of the nursing-home patient and his/her spouse were exhausted, the family would often turn to Medicaid, the federal health program for the impoverished. During the last few years many insurance companies have begun to offer policies to offset the costs of entering a nursing home or receiving long-term care.

## HOW DOES A LONG-TERM-CARE (LTC) POLICY WORK?

Long-term-care policies pay a predetermined daily benefit, after a waiting period, for a prearranged length of time. For example, a policy may contain a $100/day benefit after a thirty-day waiting period for no longer than five years.

## HOW LONG IS THE WAITING PERIOD?

Waiting, or elimination, periods on LTC policies can vary from 0 days to as many as 180 days. Generally the longer the elimination period, the lower the premium. It is important to weigh the savings of a longer elimination period against the potential cost if you should have to enter a nursing home.

## WHAT IS MY DAILY BENEFIT?

Benefits vary by policy and by insurance company. Don't rely on your insurance agent to tell you how much coverage you need. The only way you can know if the benefits in a particular policy are appropriate for your area is by doing your own research. Find out what typical nursing-home costs are in your state or town. In some parts of the country, such as New York or California, it may be necessary to have a $150/day benefit. In other states, such as Iowa or Indiana, $75/day may provide ample coverage.

## WHAT IS THE MAXIMUM BENEFIT PERIOD ON THIS POLICY?

How long is your nursing-home stay going to last? None of us knows the answer to this question. It's possible that you may spend many years in a nursing home. Insurance companies offer benefit periods that range from two years to lifetime. The longer the benefit period, the higher the premium.

## IS PRIOR HOSPITALIZATION REQUIRED TO COLLECT BENEFITS?

Most health experts recommend that a policy that requires prior hospitalization is not worth purchasing. With a disease such as Alzheimer's, for example, you may never require hospitalization. Look for a policy that does not contain this requirement.

## IS HOME HEALTH CARE COVERED?

As we discussed earlier, not all long-term care is provided in a nursing facility. Most policies will make some provision for home health care. One policy I know of even makes provisions to help modify your home to make home health care more practical (i.e, installing wheelchair ramps).

## IS THIS POLICY GUARANTEED RENEWABLE?

As with all health-insurance policies, it is important that renewability be guaranteed and that the policy cannot be canceled arbitrarily. Ask your agent to explain the conditions under which this policy could be canceled.

## CAN I PROTECT MYSELF AGAINST THE COST OF MEDICAL CARE INCREASING BEYOND MY POLICY SIZE?

Medical inflation has been running wild the last few years; the costs for hospital stays and medical procedures have been increasing at an astronomical pace. Nursing-home costs have not been exempt from these increases. Most LTC policies offer an inflation rider, which increases the daily benefit by a predetermined percentage each year.

Unfortunately, you cannot currently protect yourself against policy cost increases. Policies do not guarantee a level premium and are very likely to increase in cost each year.

# SMART QUESTIONS TO ASK ABOUT LIFE INSURANCE (with Arnold Weinstock and Roger Schilling)

It's a fact of life that we're all going to die. Most of us want to be sure that when this happens, those we leave behind are well taken care of—especially if those loved ones depend on our income to survive.

Life insurance is a contract between you and a company that says simply: You give the insurance company so much money each year (the "premium"), and in the event of your death the insurance company guarantees to pay a certain amount of money ("face amount") to someone you select ahead of time (your "beneficiary").

If you buy a $100,000 life-insurance policy, for example, you might pay a premium of $1,000 per year. Should you die at any time while this policy is in force (properly paid for and not allowed to lapse), your beneficiary would get $100,000.

Various types of life insurance can also be used for investment purposes, can be borrowed against, or can be cashed in if you're in need of emergency funds. If you have no family or business dependent on you, no desire to fund anyone or anything should you die, and no need of emergency funds, the only reason to have life insurance might be to provide burial expenses. If that's covered by other assets, you may not need life insurance at all.

## LIFE INSURANCE

### The Basics

## HOW MUCH LIFE INSURANCE DO I NEED?

There is no universal answer to this question. Your family and financial situations are different from everyone else's. Ideally, you want to protect your family both now and in the future. What would happen if you were to die suddenly tomorrow? What expenses would your family have to pay? What are your current expenses? What future expenses might you anticipate (such as college tuition, debts that may come due, and unforeseeable emergency situations)?

Make out a work sheet for yourself. On one side, figure out your income. Include your wages, commissions, bonuses, etc. Include any other sources of income you may have. Deduct the amount of taxes you pay on this income. This should give you a gross-income figure.

On the other side, figure out your expenses. Include costs of food, shelter, utilities, clothing, health care, insurance, education, child care, monthly debts (credit cards, etc.), transportation, charities—and any other debts you might have. Also, make a list of future expenses: college tuition for your kids, funeral expenses, emergency funds.

## I'VE FIGURED OUT MY INCOME AND EXPENSES. HOW DOES THAT RELATE TO HOW MUCH INSURANCE I NEED?

Generally, you want enough life insurance to replace as much of your present income as possible, or at least enough to cover your present and anticipated debts.

There are two schools of thought about how to determine the amount of life insurance you need. One school says that you want enough insurance to replace your income for a certain period of time, anywhere from five to ten years. The National Insurance Consumer Organization (121 Payne Street, Alexandria, VA 22314) recommends a period of five years. So if you were making $30,000 a year, you would multiply that number by 5 ($150,000). Then you would add on money for anticipated expenses such as college tuition and emergencies. So you might purchase a total of $250,000 to $300,000.

The second school of thought says that you want to provide a continuing supply of money for those you leave behind. Suppose you're earning the same $30,000 a year as above. What you'd like is to provide your family with enough principal so that if invested, it will produce $30,000 a year in interest. You would then purchase a policy for about $400,000. A safe investment of that money might yield 7 or 8 percent, and your family would receive about $32,000 a year.

If you're worried about your family's ability to make such an investment, you could stipulate that the insurance money be paid to a trust, with your lawyer or accountant as trustee.

## CAN I AFFORD TO BUY SO MUCH INSURANCE?

The amount of money you spend on insurance is determined more by the *type* of insurance you're buying than by the amount of coverage you get. There are many different types of insurance (which will be discussed in following questions). You don't have to buy the most costly insurance right now. You can purchase insurance that will cover your immediate needs, and then reevaluate as your income and/or your family grows.

If you've determined that you need $400,000 life insurance, there may be several different ways to get that much coverage. You must ask your agent to help you find a way. You may need to shop around, compare companies and policies.

## ONCE I'VE FIGURED OUT HOW MUCH PROTECTION I NEED, WHO DETERMINES WHAT IT WILL COST?

The insurance companies employ people called actuaries who specialize in the calculation of insurance rates. These people scientifically analyze the statistics of how many people die in this country, at each age, and for what reason, per year. This is called mortality, and actuaries use this data to establish mortality tables. These tables are modified for factors like individual health conditions, family health history, insurance-company expenses, etc., to construct insurance rates for policies.

## I'VE HEARD THE TERMS "FACE AMOUNT" AND "DEATH BENEFIT." IS THERE A DIFFERENCE?

Only a technical one: the face amount is the contractually agreed-upon amount payable to your beneficiary at the time you purchase the policy. If you buy a $25,000 policy, then $25,000, or the face amount, is payable at your death.

In subsequent years, depending on how the policy is structured, this amount might go up or down and, therefore, might be different from the original face amount of the policy. Say, for instance, your policy is designed so that dividends are used each year to purchase additional amounts of insurance. The amount of money your beneficiary would receive upon your death has now changed from the original face amount. This new amount is the actual death benefit.

## IT SEEMS THAT THERE ARE MANY DIFFERENT KINDS OF LIFE INSURANCE: TERM, WHOLE LIFE, ORDINARY LIFE, ENDOWMENT, AND MORE. IS THIS TRUE?

That's why it's so important to ask questions—you'll never know which type of policy is the best one for you unless you understand what each type of policy will (or will not) give you.

Insurance comes in two basic categories, however: term, and permanent (or cash value) policies. Term insurance is issued only for a certain length of time, and your premiums go up when the term is up.

Premiums for permanent, or cash value, insurance are higher initially, but either remain level or decrease later. These policies do not have to be renewed at higher rates after a specified period of time.

This type of policy also builds up what is known as "cash value," which means that the policy makes money for you while providing a death benefit. You can cash this policy in, if necessary, or you can borrow against it. The longer the policy is in force, the higher will be the buildup of cash in it, since more premiums will have been paid in and more earning will have been credited to the accumulation.

SMART QUESTIONS TO ASK ABOUT LIFE INSURANCE

## TERM INSURANCE

### WHAT IS TERM INSURANCE?

This is the basic policy issued by the insurance company. You pay a premium rate determined by the actuary, and you pay that rate for a specified amount of time, or "term." You can't cash this policy in at any time, nor can you borrow against it. You pay a premium for death protection only, and get nothing back unless death occurs.

### WHAT ARE TYPICAL COSTS FOR A TERM POLICY?

A $100,000 term policy from a typical insurer might cost as follows, for a male, nonsmoker:

| Age | Premium 1st Year | Premium 2nd Year |
|-----|-----|-----|
| 35 | $ 75 | $ 129 |
| 40 | 100 | 173 |
| 45 | 132 | 221 |
| 50 | 183 | 299 |
| 55 | 276 | 459 |

### WHY IS THERE A JUMP IN THE SECOND YEAR?

This is a one-year term policy and is the least expensive policy most companies issue. A one-year policy means that the premium goes up each year. Obviously, term insurance starts getting more and more expensive as you get older. Most new term contracts cannot be written after age sixty-five and most old ones cannot be renewed after age seventy.

## WHAT IS "FIVE-YEAR" TERM OR "TEN-YEAR" TERM?

When you hear a year designation in conjunction with the word "term," like "five-year term," or "ten-year term," that refers to the period during which the premium stays level. For instance, five-year term would require the same premium for each of five consecutive years, and then the premium would go up to a new level, where it would remain constant for the next five years. Ten-year term goes up in rate every ten years.

## WHAT ARE TYPICAL COSTS FOR A FIVE- OR TEN-YEAR TERM POLICY?

A woman at age thirty might pay the following premiums for a $100,000 policy for five-year and ten-year term for the first period and then the next period:

| Yearly Premium | | Yearly Premium | |
|---|---|---|---|
| 1st 5 Years | 2nd 5 Years | 1st 10 Years | 2nd 10 Years |
| $156 | $170 | $138 | $195 |

## IS A TERM POLICY RENEWABLE?

Most, but not all, term insurance is guaranteed renewable. This is a question you must ask before you purchase such insurance. If the policy is not renewable, the insurance company has the right to refuse you new insurance if you are not in good health.

Some insurers include a "right of reentry" in their term policies. This means that the insurance company has the right to recheck your health at the end of each term. It can then raise or lower your premium rates, according to your health at the time of renewal.

## WHAT IF I BUY TERM INSURANCE NOW, AND LATER ON I WANT TO CHANGE TO A DIFFERENT TYPE OF INSURANCE?

Most term policies are guaranteed convertible to cash-value-type policies. So if you want to purchase a cash-value policy, but can't afford it right now, you could buy a term policy and convert when your income improves.

## WHY SHOULD I BUY A TERM POLICY?

If you want a large amount of protection for very little cash outlay, you should buy a term policy. For instance, a young man I know, recently married, wanted a $250,000 death benefit to protect his young wife and expected child. The level cost of a ten-year term policy for him was $322.50 per year, which he felt he could afford right now. He also knew that if he wanted more protection, or a different type of policy, he could make changes later on.

Term insurance can also be used for business purposes. Two of my neighbors recently set up a small fishing-tackle shop. Each put up $25,000 to fund the business, and they resolved to sell or even give the business to their respective sons in five years. Each partner then took out $25,000 term insurance. In the event of the death of a partner, his family would get back what he had put up, and the remaining partner could continue the business. The policies cost each of the partners approximately $250 per year, level for five years.

## WHY WOULD I BUY ANYTHING ELSE, IF TERM INSURANCE IS SO "CHEAP"?

For the same reason you might buy a house, condo, or co-op rather than renting an apartment. You don't build up any equity with term insurance. Also, as you get older, term insurance can get quite expensive.

## WHOLE LIFE INSURANCE

## WHAT IS WHOLE LIFE INSURANCE?

The insurance company says basically this: If you will add additional cash to your term premium, we can invest that money (together with all the other assets of the company) in real estate, stocks, bonds, etc. In return, we will guarantee you a minimum rate of earnings on your money. If we earn more than we anticipate, we'll credit you with higher earnings. We'll fix your premium rate at the time you first buy the policy, and we will never increase your premium above that, but we could decrease it, depending on earnings and/or dividends. If it's a dividend-paying policy, we'll allow you many choices of what to do with those dividends (dividend options and policy riders will be discussed later).

Unlike term insurance, this type of insurance remains in effect for your whole life (until you die, or stop paying your premiums).

## WHAT WOULD BE CONSIDERED A GOOD POLICY OF THIS TYPE?

If you are considering a level premium whole life contract, a projection of cash values, based on the insurance company's current earnings, should indicate that you'll expect to be even after ten years. That is, your cash value will be at least equal to the sum of ten years of premium payments. If you're even after eight or nine years, or your cash value after the end of the tenth year is greater than ten years of premium payments, you have a superior policy.

The table below illustrates a projection of expected results for a policy purchased by a thirty-nine-year-old woman, a nonsmoker in good health. The face amount was $100,000.

| Year | Premium | Cash Value |
|------|---------|------------|
| 1 | $ 1,212 | $      27 |
| 2 | 1,212 | 491 |
| 3 | 1,212 | 1,539 |
| 4 | 1,212 | 2,686 |
| 5 | 1,212 | 3,949 |
| 6 | 1,212 | 5,346 |
| 7 | 1,212 | 6,896 |
| 8 | 1,212 | 8,617 |
| 9 | 1,212 | 10,535 |
| 10 | 1,212 | 12,668 |
| TOTAL | $12,120 | $12,668 |

The tenth-year cash value being a little higher than the ten years of premium payments indicates that this policy is a good one.

Keep in mind that these projections are based on a company's current earnings and expense experience, and are not guarantees. In every policy of this type there is a table of guaranteed values as well. If the company pays dividends, then the past dividend projections can be checked against actual experience to see how valid the company's projections might be.

## WHAT IS "GRADED PREMIUM LIFE" INSURANCE?

Some companies, not all, provide this type of insurance contract as an alternative to level premium whole life. The premiums for graded premium whole life start off lower than for normal whole life, and increase gradually, year by year, at a guaranteed rate.

The idea behind such a policy is to allow you to purchase whole life when your earnings do not allow a large outlay for insurance. As your earnings increase so do the premium payments, so that both the protection of the insurance and the investment or savings portion of the policy can be afforded, gradually. Younger wage earners and newly married couples generally favor this type of contract.

Below are typical costs for a $100,000 graded-premium-life-insurance policy for a thirty-five-year-old, nonsmoking, newly married male:

| Year | Premium | Cash Value |
|------|---------|------------|
| 1 | $   405 | $   10 |
| 2 | 479 | 21 |
| 3 | 553 | 285 |
| 4 | 627 | 683 |
| 5 | 701 | 1,192 |
| 6 | 775 | 1,826 |
| 7 | 849 | 2,603 |
| 8 | 923 | 3,549 |
| 9 | 997 | 4,679 |
| 10 | 1,071 | 6,021 |
| TOTAL | $7,380 | $6,021 |

## HOW DO I KNOW IF THIS IS A GOOD POLICY OF THIS TYPE?

In this type of contract, the cash value should catch up to the premium paid in somewhere between the tenth and the fifteenth years. This sample policy will have higher cash value than premiums paid after the twelfth year. While premiums will continue to increase each year, after year seven, cash value or policy equity goes up faster than the premium.

| Year | Yearly Premium | Cash Value | Cumulative Premium |
|---|---|---|---|
| 11 | $1,145 | $7,567 | $8,525 |
| 12 | 1,219 | 9,374 | 9,744 |
| 13 | 1,293 | 11,418 | 11,037 |
| 14 | 1,367 | 13,720 | 12,404 |
| 15 | 1,441 | 16,452 | 13,845 |

## WHAT IS ORDINARY LIFE?

Ordinarily, it's whole life. Some companies don't like to think of their policies as ordinary and insist that they be called "whole life," "super protector," "gladiator series," or such, but nevertheless, it's ordinary life. Whole life and ordinary life are the same, fancy names notwithstanding.

## WHAT IS AN ENDOWMENT POLICY?

An endowment policy is basically a combination insurance policy and savings plan. Like term insurance, endowment policies are purchased for a specific amount of time, called the endowment period. At the end of the endowment period, the cash value in the policy will be equal to the face amount or death protection of the policy.

For instance, you might buy a $50,000 endowment policy for twenty years, on the life of your daughter. The policy will accumulate premiums plus interest and will provide $50,000 to your daughter for tuition, travel, etc., in twenty years. But suppose your daughter does not live for the twenty years; suppose she dies accidentally after seven or eight years, what happens then? The insurance company will pay $50,000 right then and there to the beneficiary named in the policy (you, another child, or anyone you choose when you purchase the policy).

Many times, parents or grandparents buy endowment policies for children or grandchildren, guaranteeing the availability of a specified amount in, say, twenty-five years; thus you have a twenty-five-year endowment.

When my husband was ten years old, his father bought him a $5,000 ten-year endowment policy. It was designed to provide my husband with $5,000 when he reached age twenty, assuming it would pay a large part of his college expenses! Fortunately, my husband lived the ten years, and his father gave him the $5,000. Unfortunately, college costs were a bit more expensive than his father had anticipated. Premiums for endowment policies are usually expensive, so be sure you understand what you're getting and that your endowment covers cost-of-living and inflationary changes.

## ARE THERE OTHER TYPES OF LIFE-INSURANCE POLICIES?

Yes, and probably as many variations on whole life as there are companies. There's ten-pay and twenty-pay life, which require ten years and twenty years of premium pay-in respectively, at which time the policy matures. No additional premiums need be paid, the cash value and death protection continue to increase, and income can even be taken from the policy.

There are policies like life to sixty-five, life paid up at seventy-five, eighty, eighty-five, or ninety—these are policies that require premiums to be paid until you reach a certain age, after which the premiums automatically stop. If you wanted to fund your life-insurance policy while you were working, but at retirement at age sixty-five you didn't want to pay any more premiums, then life to sixty-five would be the answer. Your protection would remain in force, you could receive dividends in cash each year, and your premium-paying days would be over. Your agent can tailor-make a combination policy to suit your needs; that's what he gets paid for.

## I'VE ALSO HEARD OF VANISHING PREMIUM LIFE. WHAT IS THAT?

This refers to a policy that is structured so that you pay premiums for just a short period of time, and then never have to pay anything thereafter. How much you pay, and for how long, depends on the type of policy used; most often you would pay premiums into a whole life policy for six to eight years.

This is achieved through a process too complex to get into here. Basically, you have to pay enough cash into the policy so that after some period of years, the combination of policy earnings and dividends are sufficient to pay all future premiums. The more you put in to begin with, the sooner this point will be reached and your premiums will disappear.

## CAN ALL POLICIES BE PAID FOR BY VANISHING PREMIUMS?

No, not at all. Term insurance, having no cash value, can't be vanished. Your agent and insurance company have to work out the right policy for you so that dollars available for premiums, protection, and time period all mesh properly to meet your needs.

## HOW DO I KNOW WHEN MY PREMIUMS WILL VANISH?

Your agent will show you a projection chart that will give you an estimated idea of when your premiums will vanish. The anticipated results have to be projected by the insurance company assuming a reasonable rate of return on their investments and the size of their dividends (if any). After all, it is very difficult to say exactly what will happen during the ten or fifteen years in the future during which you'll be paying premiums.

When projections are made using conservative assumptions and factors, you can rely more safely on them. If the projection works at an anticipated rate of 7 or 8 percent, you could consider it reliable. It always pays, however, to play it safe. Some agents tell their clients that if the projection shows a vanish after eight years, pay the premium anyway in the ninth year, just as a precaution. Should the policy earnings rate or dividend scale get reduced, you might have to add some money later on anyway. On the other hand, should the earnings or dividends go up, you could obtain a vanish situation a year or two sooner.

Your agent has to guide you. Don't be afraid to ask about the interest rate anticipated or dividend scale used and judge accordingly.

## IF I SEE A PROJECTION THAT SHOWS A 10- OR 12-PERCENT EARNINGS ASSUMPTION, CAN I BELIEVE IT?

A projection at those rates could very well be realistic, but such a projection could not be considered conservative. It is important that your agent explain this in his presentation. If you buy a policy based on a fictitious earnings rate, you'll get hurt, the agent will lose future business, and the insurance company will get a bad reputation.

## WHAT IS UNIVERSAL LIFE?

It's a catchy title for a whole life policy wherein the policy's earnings, and therefore the cash value, increase or decrease according to an index, like the treasury-bond or treasury-bill interest rate. Some insurance companies choose the consumer price index or even the Dow Jones average.

Universal life policies came out when interest rates were up at 14 to 16 percent and policyholders demanded better returns on the cash values in their life contracts. Many companies promised high rates of return that would be allowed to vary according to one index or another, but with no earnings guarantees. In other words, you were given no guarantee that your cash value would increase even at a minimum rate, but would go up or down with the index.

With interest rates dropping and these indices falling slowly ever since, many companies have stopped writing universal life policies. However, there are a number of companies who took a more conservative approach to begin with, and they still write good contracts today. If you want a policy that is interest sensitive and thereby affords you a flexible premium arrangement, then this is a type of policy you might consider.

In general, universal life offers a viable alternative to term insurance. It is possible to obtain a universal policy for the same accumulated premiums as you would pay for term insurance held for ten or more years. Yet in the same time period you accumulate cash value in the universal life contract but nothing in the term policy.

## VARIABLE LIFE INSURANCE

### SINCE I LIKE TO INVEST MONEY AGGRESSIVELY, AND SINCE I MIGHT WANT SOME LIFE INSURANCE, TOO, COULD I HAVE THE BEST OF BOTH WORLDS?

There is a relatively new animal in the insurance zoo called variable life. You can "feed" the policy different amounts of premium, even on an irregular schedule, and control the investment of the cash value into a simple money market fund, or a middle-of-the-road bond mutual fund, or you can even make it jump through hoops in an aggressive growth mutual fund. You can put this year's investment into one and next year's into another, or you can mix the investments in any given year.

Remember, however, that some investments, and especially growth mutual funds, go up and down. If the fund goes up, your cash value might rise dramatically, but in a year when such mutual funds go down, you could be bitten. You might have to feed more premiums than you expected. You should clearly understand that this type of policy is an investment in securities and not simply life insurance.

## CAN MY LIFE INSURANCE AGENT SELL ME A VARIABLE LIFE POLICY?

Your agent has to be licensed to sell securities as well as insurance in order to get it for you. If you're an investor, it should appeal to you, but it isn't for everyone. It is most applicable to defined contribution pensions or profit-sharing plans that contemplate buying insurance for the participants, yet wish to maximize investments.

## I'VE BEEN LOOKING AT SEVERAL DIFFERENT POLICIES OFFERED BY THE SAME COMPANY. ONE POLICY SEEMS LIKE A GOOD DEAL, BUT ANOTHER APPEARS TO BE "NO BARGAIN." IS THIS POSSIBLE?

It is not only possible, but in fact fairly usual, to find one or two outstanding policy series within a company's portfolio, while others are just okay. For instance, some companies can sell very inexpensive term policies because the assets devoted to backing up that series are aggressively invested, and the actuarial factors used for establishing the premium rates are somewhat optimistic. By comparison, that company's whole life contracts might be very conservatively priced, based on investments tied up over a long period of time in relatively low-yielding securities. A term policy from this company might be a very good deal, but you should shop elsewhere if you needed whole life.

## LIFE INSURANCE FOR MYSELF, MY FAMILY, AND MY BUSINESS

### SHOULD I CONSIDER LIFE INSURANCE FOR MYSELF, EVEN THOUGH I'M SINGLE?

If you're young and in relatively good health, your insurance rates will be lower than they may be later on in life. So it might be a good idea to take out life insurance now, even if you're not married—and especially if you anticipate getting married and having a family someday. You also may want to consider life insurance if you are in business for yourself, or if you anticipate any business deals. Another reason to take out a policy might be to use life insurance as a "forced savings" vehicle for you to accumulate cash for retirement.

### I'M THE BREADWINNER OF THE FAMILY. SHOULD I BUY A POLICY ON MY SPOUSE'S LIFE?

In the insurance business this is called "wife insurance," but it actually applies to a man or a woman—whichever spouse is not the primary breadwinner. The spouse who does not bring in major income usually contributes to the family in many other important ways. Your spouse may be at home taking care of the children while you're bringing home a salary. If you lose your spouse, you'll still need someone to take care of your kids. Insurance money may provide you with the funds for child care while you get your life back together.

## SUPPOSE MY HUSBAND AND I BOTH WORK—SHOULD WE BOTH HAVE LIFE INSURANCE?

If the family finances depend on both incomes, if there's a mortgage to pay on either a house or a co-op, or if children are involved, it is probably a good idea. You want to be sure that the surviving spouse has enough money to take care of all the expenses you now have, plus any debts that may have accrued.

## HOW CAN I PROTECT OR INSURE MY CHILDREN'S EDUCATION?

Buy the policy on your own life, with your child or an education fund for your child as the beneficiary. Now you can build up cash, or equity, in the policy for your use later when you need money for tuition. If you aren't there to see your child go to college, the death protection of your policy will still make it happen. In other words, the cash value in the policy grows to provide the "living benefit": the money for the tuition. But if you die prematurely, the death benefit provides that same money.

## COULD I BUY AN ENDOWMENT-TYPE POLICY WHICH MIGHT BUILD UP CASH FOR SAY TWENTY YEARS IN THE CHILD'S NAME, FOR THE SAME PURPOSE?

Yes, you could. But there is an option available that may add a safety factor called a "payor benefit." This insures *you* so that in the event of your death or disability, the payments for the child's policy will continue to be made by the insurance company. While perfect for a child's endowment, this payor option is available on any policy whereby one buys a policy, or pays for a policy, for another. It is usually found when parents or grandparents pay for children's policies.

## DO YOU MEAN THAT THE LIFE-INSURANCE COMPANY WILL PAY MY PREMIUMS FOR ME IF I'M DISABLED?

Most life-insurance companies have a rider available so that, for a relatively small charge, in the event of a total disability, you need no longer pay the premiums for the policy. The company pays them instead, and the policy's equity keeps building. There are some age limitations and health requirements involved, but for the most part this benefit, called "waiver of premium," is readily available.

## COULD I HAVE THIS WAIVER-OF-PREMIUM BENEFIT EVEN IF I BUY TERM INSURANCE?

So long as the company that issues your term policy has this rider available, the answer is yes. The cost for such a rider is proportionately more expensive for a term policy, however, since the basic premium for term insurance is lower than for whole life; therefore the cost for the rider is a larger percentage of the whole premium.

Some policies will not only pay for themselves in the event of disability, but if the disability is truly permanent, after a stated number of years, the company will convert the term insurance to whole life, and will give you a completely paid-up contract from which you might borrow cash for expenses! Then you will not have to pay premiums anymore, and in addition you will receive income.

## MY SPOUSE AND I JUST SAW A HOUSE WE'D LIKE TO BUY. I KNOW WE'D NEED HOMEOWNERS INSURANCE, BUT DO WE NEED LIFE INSURANCE AS WELL?

Suppose you buy that house and after your down payment, you borrow $150,000 from a bank for your mortgage. Depending on your interest rate and duration of the mortgage, your monthly payments would average around $1,000 per month. Could you afford these mortgage payments if your spouse died suddenly? With $150,000 of life insurance on your spouse, you could pay off the mortgage and own the house free and clear.

## BOTH MY HUSBAND AND I WORK. WHOM SHOULD WE INSURE IF WE'RE GOING TO BUY THAT HOUSE?

I would suggest a policy for each of you, and for the size of the mortgage. The normal "mortgage" insurance policy is a decreasing term policy, such that the premium stays level (as opposed to regular term insurance, where the premium gets higher every year), but the protection drops off gradually as the mortgage is paid off.

## IF WE BOUGHT A POLICY TO PROTECT AGAINST OUR MORTGAGE PAYMENTS, WHAT WOULD HAPPEN IF WE MOVED?

Don't forget, the policy is on your life, not on your house. If you sell the old house and buy a new one, you would pay off the old mortgage and arrange for a new one on the next house. While you might need more insurance for the new house, you certainly can still use the old policy. You own it. It doesn't travel with the house.

## DO I NEED LIFE INSURANCE IF I'M GETTING DIVORCED?

If you're paying alimony, you do. I guarantee your spouse's attorney will insist on it, for very obvious reasons. In the event of your demise, insurance guarantees the continued flow of payments for spouse and child support, whether the divorce is amicable or hostile. Insurance might also be required to pay off the mortgage so that the family might live without the threat of losing the house hanging over their heads during this difficult time.

## I OWN A SMALL BUSINESS. SHOULD I CONSIDER LIFE INSURANCE?

Perhaps your business is a one-person show, or perhaps there's just you and a single office employee, a bookkeeper-secretary. While you make your living from this business, could your spouse run it in the event of your death? My plumber recently died, in exactly the same circumstances. His wife could not run his business, and he didn't have anyone else to take over.

Fortunately, several years ago, the business bought a large policy on his life, which allowed his wife to bridge the gap before she could sell off the business assets: pipes, tools, machines, and office equipment. She was able to pay the office person's salary for six months as well, to wind things up properly.

## I HAVE A PARTNER IN MY BUSINESS. DO I STILL NEED INSURANCE?

Since you have a partner, both of you are no doubt responsible for certain duties or aspects of the partnership. Maybe you're Ms. Inside and your partner is Ms. Outside. If Ms. Outside has a fatal accident, could you continue the business as the inside and outside person, or would you have to hire and train a new Ms. Outside? Life insurance owned by the partnership could make funds available to hire the replacement, or until a new Ms. Outside might buy into the business.

Most likely you would consider buying enough insurance so that a reasonable sum for your partner's share of equity in the business could be paid to her family, and additional money would also be available to hire someone until a new partnership arrangement might be made.

## SUPPOSE OUR BUSINESS, ALTHOUGH SMALL, IS SET UP AS A CORPORATION. DO MY PARTNER AND I STILL NEED LIFE INSURANCE?

You and your partner are now shareholders, and according to your shareholders agreement (which your attorney should have drawn up for you), you have to evaluate what your stock in the company is worth.

You and your partner have to agree that your interest in the business is worth so much, should one of you wish to sell out, and so much should one of you die prematurely. These amounts might be the same or they might be different. It is probably a good idea to insure each other for the value of your stock so that you, as the surviving shareholder, could redeem the deceased shareholder's stock easily from his estate.

## DOES IT MATTER HOW MANY STOCKHOLDERS ARE INVOLVED IN THE BUSINESS? WOULD YOU GET INSURANCE FOR ALL OF THEM?

Yes, in companies with anywhere from five to fifty partners, not large publicly held corporations. Policies could be bought by the company on each individual life, and if and when anyone dies, his or her shares could be redeemed readily by the company, as agreed upon. There need be no interruption in the business.

## WHEN DOES A BUSINESS BUY THE INSURANCE AND WHEN DO PARTNERS BUY INSURANCE ON EACH OTHER?

Just as a rule of thumb, when there are two, three, and sometimes four partners or shareholders in the business, it makes more sense for the individuals to buy the insurance on each other. This is called "cross purchasing" the policies. This way, the partners' new share of the business, after buying the deceased partner's portion from his or her estate, can be handled more advantageously from a resale point of view.

In partnerships of five or more people, it's much easier to let the business buy the insurance, own it, and be the beneficiary. In the event of a death, that individual's share is simply redeemed by the company, and is then retired (becomes treasury stock).

## CAN I GET LIFE INSURANCE THROUGH MY PLACE OF BUSINESS?

Many times you can, and there are several different ways to do so. Most large offices (from fifty to several hundred employees) have group life-insurance programs. After you've been employed a short waiting period, usually three months, you may sign up for the program. If the employer doesn't pay for it as a fringe benefit, your premium will be withheld from your paycheck, most often on a monthly basis. You'll be offered a choice of policy size, since these plans most often relate the amount of insurance to your annual salary on some schedule that allows you to choose the amount you want or can afford.

The advantages of these programs are that you get low-cost term insurance at even lower rates because the premiums are discounted for group rates. Also, due to the size of the group being covered, you may be able to get this insurance without having to answer the type of health questions usually asked before you can purchase individual life policies.

## SUPPOSE MY FIRM IS SMALLER, WHAT THEN?

While very large groups get breaks just because they're so large, small groups of employees can still buy group life insurance at affordable rates. The rates might be a little higher in a smaller company because the risks for the group aren't spread as well as with the larger group.

## WHAT IF I'M EMPLOYED IN A SMALL OFFICE THAT DOESN'T HAVE A GROUP LIFE PROGRAM? NOW WHAT CAN BE DONE?

Your relationship to the firm becomes the important consideration in this case. You and the company can join together to buy a policy on your life, and whether you live or die, each of you will get back an amount commensurate with what you put in. The technique is called "split dollar," and you do just that: you split the cost of the insurance, and you split the benefits according to the agreement that is set up.

## HOW DOES A SPLIT-DOLLAR APPROACH WORK?

Suppose you want a $100,000 policy, payable to your spouse and family should you die. You could purchase an inexpensive term policy, providing a death benefit of

$100,000 for you, at a cost of $400 per year. You'd rather purchase a whole life policy, with premiums of $2,000 per year—but you can't afford to lay out that kind of money. You could go to your employer and propose that you'll contribute $400 to the policy if your company will put in the remaining $1,600.

What does your company get out of this? You (and your agent) can set up a policy that says that, should you die, your spouse will get $100,000 and your company will get back the $1,600 it paid out per year, plus, if desired, an additional amount equal to what it would have earned on the $1,600 per year if it left it in the business (the cost of money). That way, you get the coverage you need, and the company gets its investment returned.

## SUPPOSE I QUIT OR GET FIRED, WHAT HAPPENS?

As long as your employer gets back his cash or equity, then you can keep the policy for your own purposes. The split-dollar agreement can be voided and all future premiums will be billed to you.

Your agent should be trained to handle the mechanics of all this. She will explain how you can pay the cash to your employer, either by borrowing it out of the policy (at a low interest rate) or by writing a check from your own account. Many types of arrangements can be worked out with your agent's assistance.

## IS SPLIT DOLLAR RESTRICTED TO EMPLOYER-EMPLOYEE COMBINATIONS?

No, not at all. You could have a wealthy relative helping with the equity portion of the premium payment. A trust could enter into such an arrangement—practically anyone or any entity that has a business or personal relationship to you or your spouse could enter into a split-dollar arrangement to help you get the insurance.

## I'VE HEARD THE PHRASE "KEY MAN" OR "KEY PERSON" INSURANCE. WHAT DOES THAT MEAN?

If you are very important to the operation of your company, if your input is vital to the success of the business, if your managerial skills or financial acumen play a large role in your firm's profitability, then you are a key person. (Even if you're a woman, you are still referred to in many policies as a key man.)

What would it mean to the business if you died in an accident tomorrow? If the business owner or the stockholders think you're important enough, perhaps the purchase of a very large policy on your life, *payable to the business* in the event of your loss, might go a long way in overcoming that loss until you can be replaced. If it is desired to provide additional death benefits to your family as well, using the same policy, then the premiums could be paid on a split-dollar basis.

# LIFE INSURANCE AS A SAVINGS VEHICLE

## THE BASICS

## WHAT IS LIFE INSURANCE AS A SAVINGS VEHICLE?

It is insurance like any other insurance—a benefit paid to a beneficiary as a result of a loss. Life insurance used as a savings vehicle is not purchased to make someone economically whole after a loss, however, but to create an asset to be used for some useful purpose.

## WHAT MIGHT BE A SPECIFIC EXAMPLE OF LIFE INSURANCE USED AS A SAVINGS VEHICLE?

Traditionally, you insure your life to make sure that your loved ones are provided for when you die. When you buy life insurance as a savings vehicle, you still want to see that those you care about are taken care of in the event of your death, but you also want to take care of yourself and your loved ones *during* your lifetime. In that case, you might use life insurance to pay for your children's education, your retirement, for tax purposes, or for a variety of other reasons.

## WHAT ARE SOME OF THE REASONS FOR PURCHASING LIFE INSURANCE AS A SAVINGS VEHICLE?

1. To save for college education
2. To save for retirement
3. For business planning
4. For estate preservation
5. For charitable giving

## SHOULD I REALLY BUY INSURANCE TO COVER THESE NEEDS?

Basic insurance needs should be met first. As important as saving for retirement might be, it would be wrong to purchase a whole-life-insurance policy that accumulates significant cash for retirement, but has an inadequate death benefit.

## WHAT TYPES OF POLICIES ARE APPROPRIATE AS SAVINGS PLAN?

This is not meant to be an exhaustive list of every type of contract and its nuances. It is intended as a checklist for you to use in listening to what your agent has to say:

**Term Insurance:** not applicable for saving as it generates no cash value.

**Ordinary or Whole Life Insurance:** develops cash value, therefore is appropriate for saving money. From an investment perspective, this policy should be considered the most conservative. An investment in this policy would be analogous to an investment into a regular bank savings account. It has the most guarantees as to principal and interest, but has the lowest rate of return.

**Universal Life Insurance:** develops cash value, therefore is appropriate for saving money. An investment in this contract would be analogous to an investment into a money market fund. While still considered to be a conservative investment, this type of policy allows for fluctuations in its cash surrender value to a greater degree than an ordinary life contract.

**Variable Life Insurance:** develops cash value, therefore is appropriate for saving money. An investment in this contract would be analogous to buying mutual funds, and requires the highest level of expertise upon the part of your agent. Before he can even discuss this type of contract with you, your agent must be licensed with the National Association of Securities Dealers. Variable life insurance offers a full array of investment possibilities, from simple money market funds to aggressive stock-based growth funds. You must have a very high degree of personal knowledge concerning investments or a similarly high degree of confidence in your agent.

## WHY USE LIFE INSURANCE AS A SAVINGS PROGRAM AT ALL?

The one great advantage is that while you are saving money, *you are still purchasing life insurance.* Suppose you put $100 a month into a bank savings account for the purpose of your child's education. After two years, you unexpectedly pass away. What have you accumulated? $2,400, plus a small amount of interest.

What if you put $100 a month into a $100,000 whole life policy for your child's education and you die after two years? You have accumulated a small amount of cash value for your $2,400—but your child gets the $100,000 death benefit.

## SAVING FOR EDUCATION

### IF I WANT TO USE INSURANCE TO SAVE FOR MY CHILDREN'S EDUCATION, WHEN SHOULD I START SAVING?

You should begin your savings program as early as possible. One thing to remember about using insurance for savings is that most insurance products accumulate money slowly. You need an average of fifteen years for a contract to really develop. If you wait until your child is ten years old, you'll only have eight years or so before he starts college, which may not be enough time to build your savings.

### WHAT TYPES OF POLICIES MIGHT I USE TO SAVE FOR MY KIDS' EDUCATION?

One choice might be to purchase a universal life policy, which could be compared with a money market investment. It's a fairly conservative investment, with little fluctuation in value. If the insurance company projects a 9-percent rate of interest, it will probably never fall below 8 percent.

But suppose your child is ten years old and you've just started saving for her education. You've got a long way to go and a short time to get there. In this case you might want to purchase a variable-life-insurance contract, which allows you the opportunity for investments designed to give you an enhanced rate of return.

The difference in the two types of life policies is the same as the difference between a money market and a mutual fund. If you put $50,000 into a money market account (or a universal life policy) expecting to earn 8-percent interest, and you only earn 7 percent, your $50,000 is still going to be there—plus whatever interest you've earned. If you invest $50,000 in a mutual fund (or a variable life contract), and are involved in a stock-market crash, you could end up with only $10,000 or $20,000.

## THIS SOUNDS LIKE SOME PRETTY SOPHISTICATED INVESTMENT STRATEGIES. ARE INSURANCE AGENTS EQUIPPED TO HANDLE THIS KIND OF THING?

The National Association of Security Dealers, which regulates the sale of securities in this country, requires that an insurance agent must be licensed by them before she can even talk to you about variable life insurance. Not all insurance agents have these licenses.

Before you begin discussions with your agent about this type of investment, ask about her qualifications. Also ask about her experience. You probably don't want to do business with an agent who has not had at least five years' experience with these complex policies.

## ASSUMING I LIVE TO SEE MY CHILDREN START COLLEGE, HOW DO I GET MY MONEY OUT OF THE POLICY TO PAY EXPENSES?

Essentially there are three ways:

1. You can surrender the policy and have the insurance company send you a check for the proceeds. In essence, you are telling the insurance company that

you no longer want the death benefits, because in fact you have lived long enough to accumulate the cash you need to pay for your child's education. You've met your goal, which was to save enough money to pay for tuition costs.

2. You can borrow against the cash surrender value of this policy. This would be analogous to a "passbook loan" from a savings bank, where you are in effect borrowing your own money (i.e., the bank holds your passbook as collateral, and gives you an attractive rate of interest because their risk is low).

   The advantage to obtaining the needed tuition money this way is that the life-insurance policy is still in force, so that in the event of your death, the full face amount—minus the loan (there are some ways to insure you receive the whole face amount; ask your agent to explain)—is still payable to your beneficiary. This is a loan, however, so even though you borrowed the money from yourself, it has to be paid back with interest if you are to keep the full face amount of the death protection in force.

3. Instead of completely surrendering the policy or creating a loan, you can partially surrender the policy.

   For instance, suppose you need $5,000 for the first year's tuition. If the face amount of the policy is $100,000, you would instruct your agent to surrender a portion of the policy, and reduce the face amount. You would get the $5,000 in cash, and your policy would have a new lower face amount of $90,000. This process could be continued each year until graduation day. You could continue this process until you have paid off the tuition, or until you've surrendered the entire policy.

## IF I HAVE MORE THAN ONE CHILD, SHOULD I BUY A SEPARATE POLICY FOR EACH CHILD?

Probably not. Every time you buy a new policy, you pay a new acquisition cost—the cost involved in setting up the contract on the insurance company's computer system. And every time you buy a new policy, you pay the agent a new commission. If you can cover your needs by expanding an existing policy (most policies do allow for expansion), you can save yourself money.

## HOW DO I ACCOUNT FOR INFLATION WHEN I'M PLANNING FOR MY CHILD'S EDUCATION?

You're going to have to do some homework before you see your insurance agent. Talk to various educational institutions. Most colleges have very sophisticated financial-aid services, and can give you an idea of what education costs are today, and what they're going to be in the future.

Once you've done that homework, you're ready to talk to your insurance agent. Then you can say, "I'll need $200,000 to send all my kids to college. How can I best save for that $200,000 over the next fifteen years?"

Find out what your agent's recommendations are, then go talk to your stockbroker, who is going to look at your situation from another angle. Your agent and your broker may have conflicting opinions. You'll have to decide which route is the best for you to take. You may end up putting some of that money into insurance and some of it into stocks or other investments.

## I FIGURE MY KIDS' EDUCATION WILL COST ME SOMEWHERE BETWEEN $40,000 AND $100,000. WHAT WOULD THAT COST ME EVERY MONTH?

There is no universal answer to this question. There are a number of mathematical techniques that are used to estimate how much has to be put away today based on the amount of money you wish to accumulate, your current age, and your current death-protection needs. Your agent should be able to show you all these figures before you purchase any insurance. The table below will give an idea of what these costs might be:

| Representative College Cost | Amount of Annual Savings Required to Accumulate Given College Cost Assuming 6% Interest | | |
|---|---|---|---|
| | 10 yrs. | 15 yrs. | 20 yrs. |
| $ 30,000 | $2,147 | $1,216 | $ 770 |
| 70,000 | 5,010 | 2,837 | 1,796 |
| 110,000 | 7,873 | 4,458 | 2,822 |

## DOES MY AGE INFLUENCE THE KIND OF INVESTMENT I'LL HAVE TO MAKE INTO A POLICY TO SAVE FOR MY CHILD'S EDUCATION?

As with any kind of insurance, the older you are, the higher the cost of the insurance. Many people are having children later in life. There can be a big difference in the cost of insurance if you're thirty years old and your child is two than if you're forty-five years old and your child is two. If this is your situation, you have to look very carefully at insurance as a pure investment program. Essentially, the older you are, the less attractive life insurance becomes as an investment vehicle.

## SAVING FOR YOUR RETIREMENT

## DO I NEED TO SAVE FOR MY RETIREMENT?

This is a question you need to ask yourself before you see an insurance agent. We all have heard stories of the elderly experiencing financial difficulties, from paying doctor bills to meeting rising property taxes. Add to that the breakdown in the traditional family structure, which historically acted as a support structure for the elderly. Can you see yourself in any of the above situations? What are your current circumstances? What are your projections for the future?  These are questions to help you start preparing for your future today.

## IS SOMEONE ELSE ALREADY PROVIDING FOR MY RETIREMENT?

Yes, the federal government provides for retirement benefits in the form of Social Security benefits.

## DO I NEED TO SAVE FOR MY RETIREMENT IN ADDITION TO WHAT IS BEING PUT ASIDE FOR ME IN THE FORM OF SOCIAL SECURITY BENEFITS?

YES! YES! YES!  The goal of the Social Security system is to provide a safety net to catch members of our society who, through hardship or lack of foresight, do not adequately prepare for their retirement, illness, or disability. Social Security is not intended to provide adequate income to live on in retirement; it was never intended for this purpose.

## WHO ELSE MIGHT BE SAVING FOR MY RETIREMENT? DOES MY EMPLOYER HAVE A RETIREMENT PLAN?

This is a very important question for you to ask. Not only must you know whether or not you are covered under an employer-sponsored program, you must also understand what type of plan it is and how its potentially complicated rules work. Ask your boss!

Assuming she says you are covered under a plan, you

must find out how it works. The first step is to ask for a copy of the "summary plan description." Your employer is required by law to provide you with this document, as most plans fall under federal pension regulations.

## DO I NEED TO SAVE FOR MY RETIREMENT IN ADDITION TO WHAT MY EMPLOYER IS DOING FOR ME?

The answer to this is complicated. First, read your summary plan description. Will you fulfill the requirements of the plan so that you will in fact receive the benefits promised? For example, will you work for your employer long enough to "vest" or own the benefits being promised you? Most employers require between five and ten years of service before you own, or become vested, in your benefits.

Next you must determine whether or not the amount of benefit you expect to receive, along with Social Security benefits, is enough on which to retire comfortably. An insurance agent should be able to help you work through this process.

## SOME EMPLOYERS OFFER A 401-K PLAN. WHAT IS THAT?

A 401-K plan is a special type of profit-sharing plan that allows you to set money aside on a tax-deferred basis for your retirement. Typically, you would elect to have a percentage of your regular paycheck withheld each week and set aside for you in a tax-deferred savings account to be made available to you at your retirement.

If such a plan is available to you, it might be a better option than an insurance savings plan. Remember, an insurance agent's business is to sell insurance. It's not his obligation to ask if you turned over every other stone prior to coming to him to solve your problem.

## WHAT DOES IT MEAN TO HAVE MONEY SET ASIDE ON A TAX-DEFERRED BASIS?

As you are already painfully aware, Uncle Sam gets first crack at your paycheck. A 401-K plan allows you to skim off some percentage of your paycheck before Uncle Sam gets there so that you get taxed only on what's left after your 401-K contribution has been deducted. The reason this is tax deferral, not tax avoidance, is that ultimately this money gets taxed when it is taken out for retirement purposes.

## AREN'T THERE STRINGS ATTACHED TO AN EMPLOYER-SPONSORED 401-K SAVINGS PLAN?

While there are various rules and regulations associated with gaining access to your money, essentially you are always 100 percent vested in your 401-K account. In other words, if you should leave the employ of your company for any reason (you get fired, you quit, or get laid off) the company has to give you back the money you have invested out of your own paycheck, as well as the interest it earned.

There is, however, a 10-percent penalty for withdrawal prior to age fifty-nine and a half, which you pay to the government. With the 401-K plan, the government is providing you with an incentive to save for your retirement, but it wants you to leave the money in the bank until you reach retirement age. Therefore, money that you choose to set aside into a 401-K account should be considered to be permanent savings, not short-term savings like Christmas club or money to use for your next vacation.

## WHAT DO I DO IF I DO NOT HAVE EITHER A 401-K PLAN OR SOME OTHER TYPE OF EMPLOYER-SPONSORED PLAN?

Assuming neither you nor your spouse (if you have one) is covered by a qualified retirement plan (and even that is not a problem depending on the amount of income you earn) you should consider an individual retirement account. An IRA allows you to put money into a savings account and take a tax deduction for the amount you set aside, up to approximately $2,000. The IRA also allows you to shelter the income earnings from taxation. This means that you do not have to report and pay taxes on the interest earnings paid to you.

## WHY SHOULD I OPEN AN IRA ACCOUNT INSTEAD OF INVESTING IN AN INSURANCE CONTRACT?

Basically the answer is the same as why you want to participate in a 401-K plan. Contributions are tax deferred. As a result of the tax deductibility of the contribution into the IRA, as well as the tax-free accumulation in the account, you will accumulate more money faster for your retirement.

## WHY WOULD I CONSIDER BUYING AN INSURANCE POLICY AS A RETIREMENT SAVINGS PLAN?

Not everyone qualifies for an IRA account. For example, if you or your spouse participate in a pension plan at work, you are disqualified from having an IRA. And of course, if you need life insurance protection in addition to saving for retirement, a savings-oriented life-insurance policy might be a good investment for you.

## IF I AM A SMALL-BUSINESS OWNER OR AM SELF-EMPLOYED, HOW CAN I PROVIDE FOR MY OWN RETIREMENT?

One way you can do it is through a qualified pension plan. In such a plan, the money going into the plan, and the interest earned on that money, are deferred from taxation until your retirement.

For example, suppose your company earns one dollar, which you draw out as salary. That dollar is now subject to taxation: out of the dollar, thirty to forty cents are going to be paid in taxes. In a qualified plan, instead of paying that dollar to yourself as income, you pay it into the plan as a contribution, and that dollar is not subject to taxation. So now you've got a savings plan with one dollar in it that's going to grow with interest over time, as opposed to a savings program that starts with sixty cents.

## IS THE PENSION PLAN THE MAIN VEHICLE FOR RETIREMENT?

Pension plans today are the main vehicle for the self-employed. Most of the other savings devices have been rendered useless because of government regulations.

## SHOULD LIFE INSURANCE BE PART OF THIS QUALIFIED PLAN?

By including life insurance as part of your qualified plan, the dollars used to pay the premiums are not taxed.

## WHAT ARE THE ADVANTAGES OF HAVING A PENSION PLAN FOR MYSELF AND MY EMPLOYEES?

The primary advantage is that the money invested is tax deferred. Another key advantage for the small-business person is that, for the most part, those retirement dollars are protected from bankruptcy. If you should get into trouble and go into bankruptcy, you could face a judgment that would take away your assets. In most cases your retirement dollars are safe from those judgments.

One great advantage of having a pension plan is that you are making an investment in your employees' goodwill and loyalty to the company. Most employees nowadays want to know if they're working for a company that has a retirement program. If you're going to try to retain good people, you should probably make provisions for this.

## AS A SELF-EMPLOYED PERSON OR A CORPORATION, WHAT ARE THE DISADVANTAGES FOR ME IN A RETIREMENT PLAN?

There are significant disadvantages. You must include your employees in the plan, and that may incur an expense that offsets the tax savings.

Another disadvantage is that once this money has been put into a pension plan, it is no longer available to you (until you reach the age of fifty-nine and a half) without stiff penalties. Money that goes into this qualified plan is not accessible to you for paying bills or in case of emergency.

In essence, the government makes a deal with you. It allows you to put money away on a tax-deferred basis, because it believes that if you are not given an incentive to save for your retirement, you won't. So it provides the tax-deferment incentive. The downside of the deal is that you can't take the money out before retirement, or you pay the taxes plus 10-percent interest.

One other disadvantage is that government regulation in this area has tended to become more and more burdensome over the past few years. Therefore, administrative costs associated with meeting government regulations have become more difficult and more expensive to run each year.

## IS MY INSURANCE AGENT THE BEST PERSON TO GO TO WHEN CONSIDERING A PENSION PLAN?

If he has expertise in this area. Your accountant can also be a good source to help you with this, if she is knowledgeable about pension plans.

## SUPPOSE I DON'T WANT TO BUY LIFE INSURANCE AS PART OF MY SAVING FOR RETIREMENT. DOES THAT MEAN I CANNOT DO BUSINESS WITH MY INSURANCE AGENT?

No. Most agents can offer you a pure savings plan called an annuity.

## WHAT'S AN ANNUITY?

An annuity is another kind of savings vehicle. Instead of paying a death benefit to your beneficiaries, an annuity pays you a monetary benefit during your lifetime. It also allows you to save on a tax-deferred basis. It is a way of turning cash into a guaranteed income stream. You pay in premiums over time, or all at once.

Finally, when you need the money for retirement, one of the contract's options is to guarantee a specific monthly payment for as long as you or your spouse lives.

## WHAT TYPES OF ANNUITIES ARE AVAILABLE?

Once again, this is not meant to be an exhaustive list discussing every type of contract and its nuances. It is intended as a checklist for you to use in listening to what your agent has to say:

*Fixed Annuity:* generally refers to an annuity that pays a specified rate of interest, usually set by the insurance company once a year with a guarantee of principal.

*Variable Annuity:* generally refers to an annuity that neither guarantees principal nor interest, but allows for a greater rate of return than a fixed annuity. But, buyer beware: as the annuity is allowed to increase in value, it can also *decrease* in value.

*Immediate Annuity:* can be either a fixed or variable annuity that immediately begins paying benefits to the annuitant. This would typically be bought by a person who has reached retirement and wants to begin receiving monthly payments.

*Deferred Annuity:* can be either a fixed or variable annuity that isn't expected to pay benefits until some future point in time. This annuity would typically be bought by a younger person interested in saving for retirement.

## Saving for Estate Preservation

### WHAT IS ESTATE PRESERVATION?

Estate preservation is the general term used to describe planning techniques and products whose purpose is to limit shrinkage of estate assets being passed to an heir or heirs.

### WHY IS ESTATE PLANNING NEEDED?

Federal estate tax can claim more than 50 percent of the value of an estate. This percentage doesn't include the additional expenses that also come due at that time, such as state death taxes and administrative and personal expenses. The main purpose of estate planning is to arrange your assets in a way that takes maximum advantage of the tax laws as they exist.

## HOW DOES THE FEDERAL ESTATE TAX WORK?

This tax is levied upon your right to transfer property to another person at the time of your death, and is not a tax on the property itself.

## DO I NEED ESTATE-TAX PLANNING?

A general rule of thumb might be that you do if you have an estate valued at $600,000 for a single person, and $1,200,000 for a married couple.

## IS ANYBODY ELSE DOING ANY ESTATE PLANNING FOR ME?

Yes and no. Several years ago federal regulations concerning the taxation of the transfer of assets from one person to another were changed dramatically. One such change allows you to give away your assets as a gift while you are still alive; another change allows one spouse to bequeath assets to the other spouse without a tax being imposed.

This resulted in many people making the assumption that they had in fact escaped death taxes, since all they owned could be left tax free to their spouse. In reality, all the government did was to postpone the day it would receive its due. After all, the government lives forever, but the surviving spouse has to pass away someday. And if you're single, and leave your estate to someone else in your family, you don't even have that option.

In fact, the general thrust of tax reform has been to cut

out "loopholes," leaving the average person with increased vulnerability to tax liabilities. Assuming proper steps are taken to minimize these liabilities, it may be appropriate to use life insurance to make up what cannot be planned away.

## HOW CAN I REDUCE POTENTIAL FEDERAL ESTATE TAXES?

The easiest way to reduce estate taxes is to arrange not to own anything at the time of your death. If you do not own anything at the time of your death, there is nothing to transfer to another person, therefore there is no transaction to tax.

## YOU MEAN I COULD SIMPLY "GIVE" EVERYTHING I OWN TO MY LOVED ONES AND THEREFORE ESCAPE TAXATION? WOULD THIS PLAN WORK?

NO! The problem with this thinking is that the IRS thought of it first. They have extended the idea of taxing the transfer of property from one person to another to include transfers during your lifetime, with some limited exceptions.

## WHAT ARE THOSE EXCEPTIONS?

Since the Economic Recovery Tax Act of 1981 (ERTA), you have had a 100-percent unlimited marital deduction. Thus, regardless of how much you gave or left to a spouse, it escaped taxation.

Another exception is the unified transfer credit, which applied against federal transfer taxes and is available to you, whether or not the recipient is related to you. The amount of the credit as of 1987 is $192,800, which results in the elimination of taxes on $600,000 in taxable estate assets. In addition, if you are married, you and your spouse could shelter as much as $1.2 million from all federal estate taxes.

Finally, you have the right to give any one person $10,000 per year without paying any transfer taxes. You have the right to give $10,000 to as many people as you like. If you have two children, who are both married, and each couple has two children, you could give $10,000 times six, or $60,000 per year. Additionally, if you are married, you and your spouse can each give $60,000 or $120,000. This could be done each and every year for as long as you and/or your spouse lives.

## ARE THERE ANY ADDITIONAL TECHNIQUES I SHOULD BE AWARE OF?

Wills and trusts are the legal vehicles that are used to take advantage of these loopholes. There are many possible combinations of will and trusts to accomplish most reasonable planning goals. Usually they are used in addition to life insurance and gifting programs to construct a complete plan.

## IF I CAN "SHELTER" OR "GIFT" AWAY ALL ASSETS, WHY DO I NEED TO BUY LIFE INSURANCE?

Truthfully, if you are able to do away with any potential federal-estate-tax liabilities by using the above techniques, you don't need to buy any life insurance. But things are rarely that simple. For instance, it might look good on paper to give away all your assets to reduce your tax liability to zero, but how many people would feel comfortable completely divesting themselves of all their worldly assets?

Suppose you were to give all your assets to your only

daughter, currently happily married to a most marvelous son-in-law. In the event of her premature death, all your assets (which are now her assets) become his assets. Is this really what you had in mind?

## WHAT ARE LEGITIMATE REASONS/NEEDS TO BUY LIFE INSURANCE IN CONJUNCTION WITH AN ESTATE PLAN?

An estate might have enough assets on paper to meet expenses due the government and others, but many of these assets might not be available or appropriate to pay expenses.

For example, many people have a large percentage of their total assets tied up in real estate. In fact, the family home often represents the single largest asset owned by a family. It may neither be desirable nor practical to liquidate that kind of asset to pay Uncle Sam. This is the kind of situation where large cash proceeds provided by life insurance may be the most appropriate solution.

## ARE THERE OTHER REASONS WHY I MIGHT BUY LIFE INSURANCE AS PART OF AN ESTATE PLAN?

Sometimes the division of assets among various heirs is not easily accomplished. Imagine a situation where there is a large valuable asset greatly desired by one heir, to which another heir is completely indifferent.

Suppose you have a business worth $1.5 million, plus another $500,000 in various other assets. Your daughter has been working with you for years, and has both the desire and ability to continue running the business. Your son has become a doctor and is successfully practicing in another state. He has no desire to be part of the business, but expects his fair share of the estate proceeds.

If all assets are split down the middle, each child would receive $250,000 in cash (assuming the family home is sold) plus a half interest in the business.

This may be the beginning of trouble for all. Your son's interest in the business, while valuable on paper, could mean little to him as a practical asset. After all, he can't spend it, mortgage it, or invest it.

Your daughter, on the other hand, now has a partner in what she most likely thinks of as her business. Regardless of their affection for each other, each child will have a very different perspective as to what the business should be doing.

A potential solution would be to have your daughter buy out your son's interest in the business. Where does she get the money? The first $250,000 could come from her share of the cash proceeds of the estate. She could take the $500,000 out of the business; however, most small businesses simply do not have that kind of cash around. She could borrow the money from a bank, pay her brother off, and repay the bank over time; however, this action might preclude the company from necessary future borrowing.

If, however, you purchase life insurance for $500,000 and name your son as beneficiary, he will get the cash he needs, you can then leave the business to your daughter free and clear, and both children will receive equal and fair inheritances.

## I'VE HEARD THAT I SHOULD NOT OWN THE LIFE-INSURANCE POLICY ON MY LIFE. WHAT'S THAT ALL ABOUT?

There are many considerations associated with who owns the life-insurance policy on your life. If the primary goal of your estate plan is to minimize taxes paid, someone other than yourself should own the policy. Remember, estate taxes are levied upon assets you own and transfer to another. If you never own the policy, you cannot be taxed on it.

## IF I SHOULDN'T OWN IT, WHO SHOULD?

Your first consideration might be your spouse, if you have one. This would solve the problem of keeping the asset out of your estate and does not require any complicated trusts.

Making someone else owner of a policy on your life is not without its drawbacks, however. Legally, you no longer own, or control, the policy; that's why the chosen owner is usually a spouse or some close family member. Another solution might be to have a trust own the policy. (A trust is a document that provides for a trustee—usually someone experienced in financial management—to manage the estate on behalf of the beneficiary.)

## SAVING FOR CHARITABLE DONATIONS

### SHOULD LIFE INSURANCE BE USED AS A PART OF A GIFT-GIVING PROGRAM?

The desire to give is a very personal decision. If you do wish to leave money to a religious, educational, or charitable institution, you should carefully discuss with your insurance agent whether or not life insurance is an appropriate option for you and the institution you wish to help.

### DOES MY CHARITY NEED CASH NOW OR CASH LATER (AT MY DEATH)?

An important thing to remember is that life-insurance benefits are paid only at your death. While this might be considered an overstatement of the obvious, remember that many worthy institutions need operating funds *now*.

So before discussing gift giving through life insurance with your agent, it might be very helpful to contact the proposed beneficiary first and discuss your plans with them.

## WHY SHOULD I INVEST MY CHARITABLE DONATIONS INTO A LIFE-INSURANCE CONTRACT INSTEAD OF JUST GIVING THEM THE CASH?

You may not have a large sum of money to donate right now. It may be possible for you to name the charity as beneficiary in an insurance policy that pays more than you could afford to give on your own.

## HOW ELSE MIGHT LIFE INSURANCE BE USED IN A GIFT-GIVING PROGRAM?

It is possible to use life insurance as part of a wealth-replacement program. The general concept works like this: You donate an asset to a charitable organization. In addition, you purchase a life-insurance contract in an amount equal to that which you gave away so that at your death the value of what you gave away is returned to your family.

Suppose you donated a piece of real estate with a current market value of $100,000 to a charitable organization. This could allow you a tax deduction of $100,000. If you were in a 40-percent tax bracket, this could mean a tax savings to you in the amount of $40,000—but to get it, you gave away a piece of property equal to $100,000. Therefore, you or your family are out $60,000. But if you were to purchase a life-insurance contract in the amount of $100,000, at your death your family would have the value of the property replaced.

## WHAT IF THE PROPERTY WE ARE PROPOSING TO GIVE AWAY IS OF SUCH SENTIMENTAL VALUE TO THE FAMILY THAT ULTIMATE LOSS OF IT TO THE FAMILY IS UNACCEPTABLE?

It is further possible that at the time of your death the proceeds of the insurance policy could be used to repurchase the previously donated property so that in the end the charity gets cash, and the family gets to keep its beloved heirloom.

It should be noted that there are very complicated issues involved in making any of these ideas work. Further, it would not be reasonable to expect your insurance agent to be completely equipped to handle every aspect of these transactions. You will very likely need the services of an attorney, a CPA, and maybe a bank trust officer. What your insurance agent should be able to do is help coordinate the services of these other professionals in accomplishing your goals.

## WHO SHOULD OWN THE INSURANCE CONTRACT?

If you own the contract and make the charity the beneficiary, you may lose the current deductibility of the premiums paid on its behalf. However, owning the policy allows you to exercise full legal control over the contract—such as changing the beneficiary or borrowing against its cash surrender value for personal use.

If the charity owns the policy, it could exercise all legal rights over it, but you could most likely deduct the premiums against your current income taxes. It cannot be overly stressed that your agent had best be conversant with these matters if she is going to recommend the purchase of products to accomplish these complicated goals.

# SMART QUESTIONS TO ASK ABOUT PROPERTY AND CASUALTY INSURANCE (with Donald Manning, Michael Kreps, and Robyn Reilly)

What is property and casualty insurance? Property insurance refers to protection for loss on property owned by you, or for which you may be legally responsible. Casualty refers to protection of your assets from lawsuits brought by others because of your negligence.

There are many reasons for buying property insurance. In some cases the law says that you have to buy insurance. This is the case in most states when you own an automobile. In other situations, for instance when you get a loan from a bank to buy a house, the bank will want you to have insurance to protect their interest in the property on which they have a mortgage.

Casualty insurance can protect you from liability due to your negligence—from being sued because of something you did, or neglected to do.

Often casualty and property insurance are combined to form a package policy. Most people who own a home and have what is referred to as a homeowners policy actually have a package policy.

## THE BASICS

### IF I SUFFER A LOSS, HOW DO I HANDLE IT?

At the time of the incident, remain calm and gather as many facts and bits of information as you can. If there is damage to your property, you can make any emergency repairs that you have to in order to prevent further loss. For instance, if a water pipe in your home springs a leak, you can call a plumber immediately to have the pipe fixed so that the flooding doesn't get worse.

Then contact your insurance agent or company so that they can inspect the remaining damage. If it's possible to contact your agent, do that first. The agent will then report to the company and act as an intermediary for you.

### WHAT IF THE LOSS OR ACCIDENT IS SERIOUS AND I CAN'T CONTACT MY AGENT RIGHT AWAY?

Most insurance policies require you to inform your agent of the accident, damage, or loss as soon as is reasonably possible. That does not mean that you have to call your agent the minute you discover your basement is flooded. Waiting until the following morning, or Monday morning if a loss occurs over the weekend, is acceptable in most circumstances. Good judgment and common sense are required.

## WHAT IF I CAN'T REACH MY AGENT? IS THERE ANYTHING ELSE I SHOULD BE DOING?

Many insurance companies also have an 800 number that you can call. However, that usually means the paperwork doesn't get handed down to the people who actually handle your claim until four or five days later, whereas if you wait a day or so until your agent is available, the process can get started that much sooner.

Also, the people at the 800 number are usually telephone clerks who simply report whatever you tell them. They cannot give you advice, tell you what to do, or where to go for repairs. Your agent, on the other hand, is familiar with your area and can be of great help in answering your questions.

## IS THERE A TIME LIMIT WITHIN WHICH I MUST REPORT A CLAIM?

If your property is damaged, or someone is injured in your home or on your property, contact your insurance agent as soon as possible. If you are unable to contact your agent or insurance company for a few days, your coverage would not be jeopardized. If, on the other hand, you waited months to report the incident, your company may exercise certain rights to protect its interest because of your late notification and filing. Every policy says that you have to report the claim as soon as possible.

There is usually a statute of limitations beyond which the company does not have to accept your claim. This statute of limitations is different with each insurance company (and in each state), so be sure to ask your agent about this detail in your policy. Your best protection, however, is to report an incident as soon as you possibly can.

\*   \*   \*

In this section of the book, we are covering numerous options in insurance coverage. We are not at all suggesting that you should have all of the coverages mentioned—but we wanted to let you know what is available should you need it, and the questions you might need to ask in each situation.

# AUTOMOBILE INSURANCE

## THE BASICS

### WHY DO I NEED AUTOMOBILE INSURANCE?

Automobile insurance in some form or another is mandatory in most states. Obtaining insurance also provides you with a sense of security in knowing that in the event of an accident, you are protected against financial loss.

However, an insurance policy does not give you license to drive recklessly. You should always drive defensively, and never drive under the influence of drugs or alcohol.

### ARE THERE MANY DIFFERENCES BETWEEN THE KINDS OF AUTOMOBILE POLICIES THAT YOU CAN BUY, OR ARE THEY FAIRLY STANDARD?

There are basically only two kinds of policies. The first, and most common, is an owner auto policy—when you buy insurance for a car you own.

The second is a non-owned auto policy. If you don't own a vehicle, but you often rent one, or if you have a car that's furnished for your use by your employer and you want more coverage than the company provides, you can buy a non-owned auto policy. This type of policy is not in frequent demand, and it's usually very expensive.

## HOW ARE AUTOMOBILE INSURANCE RATES DETERMINED?

There are many variables that go into rate making. The following represent the most common:

*Location of Garaging:* Areas that experience high numbers of accidents or thefts may result in higher rates.

*Driver Experience:* Inexperienced operators generally pay higher rates than experienced operators. Age, gender, and marital status also play a part in the rate-making process. For instance, unmarried males, age twenty-nine and under, pay higher rates than married males. However, an unmarried female does not pay a higher rate than a married female.

*Vehicle Use:* Vehicles used for business purposes and vehicles that are driven extensively will have higher rates than vehicles used for pleasure only or low-mileage commutation. Commuting has two classifications: ten miles and under, or over ten miles. And if you use the car three out of five days for commuting, your insurance rates are the same as if you commuted all the time.

*Vehicle Type:* High-performance vehicles, sports cars, and vehicles susceptible to high incidences of vandalism and theft will result in higher premiums than those with low incidence statistics.

*Driving Record:* Probably the most important and most controllable factor in determining insurance rates is your driving record. The better driver you are, the lower your insurance rates will be. The more accidents you have, the more premiums you will pay. The cost to you depends on the accident, and it varies from state to state. In New York, if the accident is your fault, you get surcharged 20 percent for three years. In other states, like New Jersey, for instance, there is a fee for each accident. You are charged $300 a year per accident for three years. If you have a lot of accidents, the company will probably not renew your policy because you will be deemed a high risk.

## WHAT ARE SOME TYPICAL COSTS FOR CAR INSURANCE?

It depends on all the factors mentioned earlier, including where the car is kept, what type of car it is, how old you are, and if you're married or single.

Let's take a man and woman in Westchester County in New York, for example. They have a 1990 Lexus and 1987 Cadillac. They have $300,000 liability coverage. They have $300,000 insured motorist coverage, $500 deductible on comprehensive and collision coverage. Their premium is $1,900 per year. That's very low because they've been with this insurance company for a number of years, they've maintained clean driving records, had no claims, and are over thirty.

## DOES MY POLICY COVER MY MEDICAL EXPENSES IF I'M HURT IN AN ACCIDENT?

The answer is yes, if you have personal injury protection on your policy. This covers injuries to you or to members of your family related by blood, marriage, or adoption.

Not every state has personal injury protection. For instance, New York, New Jersey, and Connecticut have this type of coverage; North Carolina, Florida, and California do not. In those states, you would be covered by your health insurance if you were injured in an automobile accident.

## WHAT IS NO-FAULT INSURANCE?

No-fault insurance is another name for personal injury protection. Check the laws of the state in which you predominantly drive to find out if you have such coverage (ask your insurance agent or call the Department of Motor Vehicles) and what that coverage includes.

Under the New York State no-fault law, for example, your insurance company pays any medical or hospital expenses and lost income immediately, without regard to who is to blame for the accident.

In some cases no-fault provides funds if you are hurt in an accident and you can't work. No-fault also covers you for death benefits if you're killed. A specified amount of money (which also varies from state to state) is paid to your surviving spouse, parents, or children. No-fault may also cover funeral expenses.

## ISN'T IT SOMETIMES DIFFICULT TO DETERMINE WHETHER OR NOT AN ACCIDENT IS MY FAULT?

Many times it is difficult to determine who is at fault. If you have an accident and you don't think it's your fault—and your insurance company agrees with you—the company will pay to have your car fixed. Then they'll turn your file over to what is called a subrogation unit. The fault will then be reexamined by the claims adjuster through a review of the motor vehicle report submitted, through a police report if available, or through witness statements.

Many states have contributing negligence laws that might hold you responsible for a portion of the claim even if you were not entirely at fault in the accident. For example, you might be in an accident at an intersection with no traffic lights or stop signs. Even though you may have had the right of way, you or your insurance company can be held liable for a percentage of the damages if it is determined that your negligence was at least 50 percent of the cause of the accident.

Subrogation means the insurance company is now going to attempt to get all the money back that they paid you, plus your deductible. The subrogation unit contacts the other driver's insurance company. If it's clearly the other man's fault, you're going to get most or all of your deductible back within one year. If it's contributory negligence, you'll get much less back.

## WHAT HAPPENS IF I HAVE SEVERAL ACCIDENTS THAT ARE MY FAULT?

If you have several accidents, moving violations, or even several comprehensive claims (thefts, fires, vandalism), you could find that standard auto insurance will not be available to you.

The alternative would be an assigned risk pool, where you would be assigned to an insurance company as a poor risk. The assigned risk policy will usually be provided by a standard company; however, the rates are higher and the policy limits are usually lower. If your record is fairly good after three years, you may then be able to reapply for standard coverage.

## ARE THERE ANY OTHER REASONS THE COMPANY MIGHT NOT RENEW MY POLICY?

A company may cancel your policy if you have a number of traffic tickets, depending on the nature of the tickets. There are two different categories of tickets. The first is for minor infractions, such as running a red light or a stop sign, or making an illegal turn. The second category is more serious. These are tickets for offenses such as excessive speeding (fifteen miles over the limit), careless driving, reckless driving, or driving while intoxicated. If you have a ticket from this category, insurance companies will probably refuse to insure you. If you get this type of ticket while you're already insured, the company may not renew your policy upon the next renewal date.

## ARE THERE ANY COMPANIES THAT WILL INSURE ME EVEN THOUGH I HAVE A FEW TICKETS?

The majority of companies will not. However, in some states, if you do other business with the company, they will also give you auto insurance. For instance, if you have a $300,000 homeowners policy with some companies, they will be more inclined to give you an automobile-insurance policy, even if you have more than one ticket. This practice is illegal in some states; you can check with your state insurance department if you have a question.

## WHAT IS BODILY INJURY LIABILITY?

Bodily injury liability provides money to pay claims that result from injuries or death to passengers in your car, to pedestrians, or to people in other cars. If any of those people hold you responsible for their medical bills, or sue you for their pain and suffering, your bodily injury coverage provides the funds to pay these damages.

Suppose that during a raging storm you lose control of your vehicle and hit the car in front of you. The people in that car sustain minor injuries and sue you to compensate for their injuries, pain, and suffering. The bodily-injury-liability portion of your insurance will cover these costs, within the limits of your policy.

## WHAT ARE THE LIMITS OF SUCH LIABILITY COVERAGE?

The minimum amount of coverage you must carry varies in each state. Ask your agent what your state requires. The minimum coverage you can obtain in New York State is $10,000 per person, $20,000 per accident.

If you were in the accident mentioned above, and you had the minimum coverage, each person injured would be entitled to receive up to $10,000. However, if there were more than two people injured, or if they sued you for more than $10,000 each, you would have to pay the difference out of your own funds, or carry umbrella coverage (see page 182 ).

## DOES MY POLICY COVER ME IF I DRIVE SOMEONE ELSE'S VEHICLE WITH PERMISSION?

You are also covered for injuries to others if you drive someone else's car with the owner's permission. Your policy also covers you if you rent a car.

## WHAT IS UNDERINSURED MOTORIST COVERAGE, AND WHY IS IT NECESSARY?

Underinsured motorist covers you if you are in an accident, and your medical costs exceed the amount of insurance carried by the other party involved. Underinsured motorist also covers guests in your car, you, and your family if riding in someone else's car or if injured as a pedestrian.

You usually purchase this coverage in an amount equal to, or less than, your bodily injury coverage. So if you have $100,000 bodily injury coverage, you would normally take $100,000 in underinsured motorist coverage.

Suppose Mr. Smith, who has $10,000 worth of insurance, hits you with his car. You break an arm and a leg, and you're in the hospital for three months, and then you have to have many more months of physical therapy. You want to sue Smith for $500,000 for your pain and suffering. This case will probably go to court, and the court will determine how much you are to receive. If the court awards you $100,000, you'll get $10,000 from Mr. Smith's insurance, and the $90,000 difference from your insurance policy.

## WHAT IS UNINSURED MOTORIST COVERAGE, AND WHY IS IT NECESSARY?

Uninsured motorist is actually part of your underinsured motorist coverage. It covers you in the event that you or a family member are injured in a hit-and-run accident or involved in an accident with an individual who has no insurance. Uninsured motorist also covers guests in your car, and you and your family if riding in someone else's car or if injured as a pedestrian.

Suppose Mr. Smith had no insurance, and the accident was caused by his negligence. You can sue, but if Smith has no money, you may be out of luck. With uninsured motorist coverage, you can collect, up to your limit, under your own policy.

## I THOUGHT IT WAS MANDATORY TO HAVE SOME INSURANCE?

Although this is true in most states, people don't always follow the rules. When you first register your car, the Department of Motor Vehicles requires proof of insurance. So you show them an insurance card, which means that you've paid your premiums.

What happens if you don't pay it your next bill, or you forget to pay your premiums, and your policy is canceled? Or what if you're in the process of getting new insurance when you have an accident?

In some states insurance companies are required to notify Motor Vehicles when a policy is canceled—but not in all states. Therefore, you may still be driving, even though your insurance is no longer intact.

## WHAT IS PROPERTY DAMAGE LIABILITY?

This provides coverage for damage that your car has caused to another person's property. You're traveling on an icy road and your car skids into a parked truck and slams into a storefront, breaking glass, twisting metal framing and making a general mess of everything. Luckily, you are not hurt, and both the parked car and the store were empty at the time. All the damage was to other people's property. You would be covered under your property damage liability, up to your policy's limits.

## WHAT IS COLLISION INSURANCE?

Collision insurance covers damage to your vehicle caused by you or by another party while you're driving your car, or while it is parked. It also covers you if you park your car and put your emergency on, but your car rolls back into another car.

This type of protection comes with a deductible clause, which means that you must pay the stated amount of money, and the insurance company will pay the balance to repair your car. If you have a $200 deductible, you pay the first $200 of the loss. This is similar to a deductible in medical insurance—except that with medical insurance the deductible is usually for each year. In automobile insurance and homeowners insurance, the deductible is $200 per occurrence. So if you have one claim today and another one next week, each one will cost you $200. The most common deductible amounts are $200, $250, or $500.

## WHAT IS COMPREHENSIVE INSURANCE?

Comprehensive insurance covers your vehicle against losses such as fire, lightning, theft, glass breakage, flood, vandalism, and various other perils (including damage caused by hitting an animal such as a deer), excluding collision or upset. There's usually a deductible on this type of coverage as well.

Suppose vandals attempt to steal your parked vehicle. Although they do not succeed, they damage the door lock, smash the windshield, break the ignition, and damage the steering column. Suppose your tires are slashed, or your car is scratched, or your car is stolen and recovered with a serious amount of damage—all these incidents are covered under comprehensive insurance.

## HOW CAN I SAVE PREMIUM DOLLARS ON MY COMPREHENSIVE AND COLLISION INSURANCE?

When you increase your deductible, your premiums go down. So you should take the highest deductible you can afford on your budget.

If your car is more than seven or eight years old, you should consider dropping your collision and comprehensive coverage. First, ask your agent to look up the book value of your car—what you would receive if your car was totaled or stolen. This valuation includes the extras you purchased (i.e., sunroof, leather seats, etc.) with deductions for excess mileage.

If the book value is $2,000 or $3,000, you may want to delete the collision and comprehensive coverage—depending on where you live and what you are paying for the coverage. If you live in New York and your collision and comprehensive coverage is $1,000 a year, and the car is only worth $2,000, it might not pay for you to keep this coverage. If you live in another state and your collision and comprehensive is $500 a year and your car's value is $3,000, then it may be worth it.

## HOW DO I DETERMINE IF IT'S WORTH IT TO PAY FOR COLLISION AND COMPREHENSIVE COVERAGE?

Check the actual cash value of your vehicle, then add up the premiums you're paying for collision and comprehensive, plus the deductible. If the total comes to more than 10 percent of the value of the vehicle, it's not worth it.

For example, if your vehicle is worth $2,000 and you're paying $150 for collision and comprehensive insurance and you have $150 deductible, for a total of $300, you should cancel your collision and comprehensive.

## IS THERE ANY SITUATION WHERE I MUST KEEP THIS COVERAGE?

If you have a loan on your car, you're not allowed to drop your collision and comprehensive coverage, and you must retain this coverage when you have a leased vehicle.

## DOES HAVING A CAR ALARM SAVE ME ANY MONEY?

You can save money on your comprehensive coverage by putting an alarm system in the car. There are two types of alarms. One is a passive alarm, which means as soon as you shut the car off, the alarm sets itself. You get credit on the comprehensive premium (which varies from policy to policy) for this type of alarm.

The other is an active alarm, which means that you have to activate it, usually by punching in a code. There's a credit, although smaller than the one you get for a passive alarm, for this type of alarm as well.

## WHAT IF I HAVE MORE THAN ONE CAR TO INSURE?

If you have more than one car on a policy, you get a discount on the second, third, and fourth vehicle. You're always better off having all your cars on one policy, so you can get that multicar discount.

## WHAT HAPPENS IF THE COST TO REPAIR MY CAR EXCEEDS THE VALUE OF THE CAR?

When this happens, the car is considered to be a total loss. Most companies will take formal possession of your car and pay you the book value of the vehicle. Some companies under some circumstances will adjust the loss to below total value, pay you this lower amount, and allow you to keep the vehicle.

## MAKING A CLAIM

## HOW DO I PUT IN A CLAIM AFTER I'VE HAD AN ACCIDENT?

Call your agent with all the details. She will then report the incident to the insurance company.

## WHO WILL HANDLE MY CLAIM AFTER IT IS REPORTED TO MY AGENT?

Your insurance company will assign a claims representative to handle your claim, and he will contact you.

## HOW MUCH TIME SHOULD I ALLOW FOR THE CLAIMS PERSON TO CONTACT ME?

Each state has different laws, but in most cases the insurance company must get in touch with you within six to seven business days. If you don't hear from anyone, call your agent again. Usually, however, the insurance company will contact you within three or four days.

## WHAT INITIAL INFORMATION IS NEEDED TO HANDLE MY CLAIM?

You must provide your full name and policy number, an accurate description of the accident including the time, date, place, and conditions under which it occurred, and the nature of any injuries.

You should also know the names, addresses, phone numbers, dates of birth, and insurance companies of any other drivers and/or passengers involved, as well as the model, make, year, and the ID numbers of other vehicles involved.

Carry an accident report form in your glove compartment, which you can get from your agent or your insurance company, or from your local Motor Vehicles or police department.

## HOW CAN I GET MY CLAIM PROCESSED AS QUICKLY AS POSSIBLE AND IN THE BEST POSSIBLE WAY?

Once a claim is reported to the company, you deal directly with a claims adjuster. If you have problems, you can always call your agent to intervene for you, but it is usually quicker if you deal directly with the company.

If your car is stolen, or if it's a total loss, you can't get paid until you submit the title of the vehicle to the insurance company. You should always know where your title is, because if you can't find it, you have to write to the state capital and order another title. That takes four to six weeks, and will delay your claim.

## WHAT IS THE EXACT PROCESS OF FILING A CLAIM?

Call your agent to report the accident. Your agent then reports it to the insurance company. The insurance company assigns your case to an adjuster. The adjuster will then contact you directly, or go to the body shop where your car is being repaired. If possible, have the adjuster contact you first so that you can keep track of the entire process.

The adjuster then goes to the repair shop to inspect the damages and write up a report. He'll usually try to agree on a price to repair the car with the body shop while he's there.

The report is submitted to the claims department of your insurance company. After reviewing the report, they issue a check, less any deductible. The check may be mailed directly to you, or it may be mailed to the agent, who then mails it to you. In certain cases you can sign an authorization that allows the insurance company to pay the repair shop directly (some body shops may require this type of payment).

## HOW LONG SHOULD THIS WHOLE PROCESS TAKE?

It should take approximately two weeks. In some instances a check can be issued at the time of the inspection of your vehicle.

## WHAT IS MY ROLE IN MAKING SURE THAT THESE THINGS HAPPEN? WHAT CAN I DO TO BE SURE THINGS RUN SMOOTHLY?

Your role is to stay on top of the process. Don't just contact your agent and wait for a check. Stay in contact with the body shop. Make sure the adjuster was there. If he wasn't, call your agent immediately.

It's a good idea to "make friends" wherever you can. Keep up a good relationship with your car repair service and with your insurance agent. You never know when you might need their help.

## WHERE SHOULD I HAVE THE CLAIMS ADJUSTER SEE MY CAR—AT MY HOME OR AT THE BODY SHOP?

You should have the claims adjuster go to the body shop or the dealer—wherever the car is being fixed. That way the adjuster can talk to the people who are actually doing the repairs, and come to an agreement about the costs of parts and labor.

## WHAT CAN I DO TO BE ASSURED THAT I GET FULLY REIM-BURSED WHEN I HAVE A CLAIM?

Don't take your car to a dealer for repairs unless it's brand new. Dealers often charge forty to fifty dollars an hour for labor; body shops usually charge between twenty and thirty. Most insurance companies pay only between twenty and forty dollars. So if you take your car to a dealer, your insurance company may not be willing to pay the dealer's charges. However, if you have a brand-new car with fewer than several thousand miles, you'll probably want to take it to the dealer so the people who sold it to you can fix it.

## WHAT IF ADDITIONAL ACCIDENT-RELATED DAMAGE IS FOUND AFTER REPAIR WORK HAS BEGUN ON MY VEHICLE?

If the repair shop finds additional accident-related damage after they've begun work on your car, or if there are any changes to the appraised amount for any reason, the repairer must contact your claims representative for approval prior to making the repairs. After your claim representative approves the additional charges, a supplemental check will be issued.

## WHAT HAPPENS IF I HAVE MY CAR REPAIRED AND SEVERAL DAYS LATER I NOTICE AN ADDITIONAL DAMAGE THAT WASN'T REPAIRED OR PAID FOR UNDER MY CLAIM?

Notify your insurance agent or company claims department as soon as it is apparent that there is an additional problem. Ask the company to send the adjuster to reinspect your vehicle in an effort to determine whether or not the additional problem is due to the previous accident. It would also help to get a written statement from your body shop or local mechanic indicating that the problem was caused by the accident.

## WHAT IF THE ADJUSTER AND THE BODY SHOP DISAGREE ON COSTS?

Submit a copy of the estimate from the body shop to the insurance company. The adjuster will look at it. If he feels it's in line, he'll readjust his appraisal. In most cases you will find the difference in labor rate is what causes the difference in opinions.

\*　　\*　　\*

## IS A CLAIMS ADJUSTER ALWAYS INVOLVED?

In certain instances, and with certain companies, you may be sent to a body shop that can make the repairs without a claims adjuster. Also, some smaller claims, such as glass, towing, or tire claims, may be handled by your agent upon presentation of a paid bill.

## HOW WILL I GET PAID?

Your claims representative will issue a check for the appraised amount, less your policy deductible. Note that if there is a lien on your vehicle—for example, if you have bank financing—the check will be made payable to you and the lien holder; they must also endorse the check.

## RENTING OR LEASING A CAR

### I WAS IN AN ACCIDENT AND MY CAR WAS A TOTAL LOSS. NOW I HAVE TO RENT A CAR TO GET TO WORK. IS THIS COST COVERED?

You can purchase rental reimbursement coverage, which is sometimes known as loss-of-use coverage. If you have a covered claim, meaning an accident or a collision, or your car is broken into and can't be driven, or it's in the shop being repaired, you can rent a car and your policy will pay you a certain amount of money per day (for a period of thirty days) to rent a replacement car. That amount ranges from ten to sixty dollars per day, depending on your policy.

### I'M RENTING A CAR FOR A VACATION TRIP. AM I COVERED?

If you rent a car from a legitimate rental company, the liability from your auto policy covers you over the limits provided in the rental agreement. If you maintain collision coverage on your policy, that also covers a rental vehicle.

In most states—but not all—the law says that your auto policy must provide coverage for a rental vehicle. However, you may not be fully covered if your insurance is for an '89 Ford and you rent a Rolls-Royce or a Ferrari.

If you have an auto policy that includes liability but not collision, you should take out collision coverage with the rental company. Some credit-card companies will also cover collision damage if you charge the rental on their card.

## WHEN DO I NEED TO TAKE FULL COVERAGE FROM THE RENTAL COMPANY?

If you do not own a vehicle or have automobile insurance, if you have a high deductible, or if you rent an exotic or high-priced car, you should take out the full coverage.

## AM I COVERED IF I RENT A CAR OVERSEAS?

The answer is no; always obtain the insurance from the rental company.

## WHAT IF I LEASE MY CAR?

By signing a lease for a vehicle, you are responsible for the value of the vehicle plus the interest on the lease over a period of time. In case of a total loss, the insurance company will only pay for the retail price of the vehicle, not the interest owed. Therefore, in most cases, you'll owe more on your lease than you'll get back from the insurance company.

## HOW CAN I PROTECT MYSELF IF I LEASE A CAR?

There is a new type of insurance called gap insurance, which provides the difference between what your insurance company pays you and what you owe on the lease. Suppose you owe $12,000 on your lease when your car is totaled. You still owe $12,000 on the lease, even if the actual cash value of the vehicle at the time is only $10,000. The insurance company would only pay you $10,000; you would still owe the leasing company the difference of $2,000. If you had purchased gap insurance (usually offered by the leasing company at a cost of several hundred dollars over a three-to-five-year lease), you would then not have to pay anything except your deductible.

## I LEASED A CAR THROUGH MY BUSINESS, BUT I WANT TO COVER IT UNDER MY PERSONAL INSURANCE. CAN I DO THAT?

No, you cannot. The insurance contract and the lease agreement have to be in the same name. A car cannot be leased to a business and insured under a personal auto policy.

## SHOULD I PURCHASE MY OWN INSURANCE FOR A LEASED CAR, OR DO IT THROUGH THE LEASING COMPANY?

Ask the leasing company if they have an insurance program and, if so, how much coverage they can provide. Sometimes this is less expensive than going through an insurance company or broker to get the coverage.

## INSURING MOTORCYCLES, MOPEDS, MOTOR HOMES, AND MOBILE HOMES

## HOW DO I INSURE MY MOTORCYCLE OR MOPED?

A moped or motorcycle policy is very similar to an automobile policy. The following coverages are mandatory:

Bodily injury liability
Property damage liability
Uninsured motorist coverage
Personal Injury Protection (optional in some states)

Comprehensive and collision coverages are optional. The limits of coverage vary depending upon the state in which the bike is garaged.

## DOES THIS COST MORE OR LESS THAN CAR INSURANCE?

Usually it depends on the type of motorcycle you buy and where you live (i.e., in a city or out in the country). If you have a motorcycle that goes extremely fast, it could cost more than auto insurance. Moped insurance is inexpensive, usually costing no more than $200 a year.

## I OWN AN ALL-TERRAIN VEHICLE (SNOWMOBILE) AND IT IS USED ON THE PREMISES AT MY HOME. DO I HAVE TO OBTAIN A SEPARATE INSURANCE POLICY TO COVER IT AND TO COVER LIABILITY?

No. As long as the vehicle is used on your property, it is automatically covered under your homeowners policy, as is the liability. If the vehicle is operated off your property, then a separate policy must be written.

## I AM THINKING OF PURCHASING A MOTOR HOME. HOW DO I GO ABOUT INSURING IT? ARE THE CONTENTS IN THE HOME COVERED?

A motor-home (one that has an engine) policy is just like an automobile policy. All coverages listed for mopeds and motorbikes are the same as well. The contents are not covered and must be added on by endorsement.

## I AM PURCHASING A MOBILE HOME AT A LAKE TO BE USED AS A SUMMER RESIDENCE. HOW DO I INSURE IT?

A mobile-home (one that has no engine and is attached to another vehicle) policy is similar to a homeowners policy. The following coverages are available: home, loss of use, personal property, and personal liability.

## INSURING YOUR BOAT

### WHAT IS BOAT INSURANCE?

Boat insurance covers the boat itself, and is usually separated into two sections; the first covers the hull and engine, and the second section covers liability.

### WHAT IS THE HULL?

The hull is the actual structure of the boat, including its sails, machinery, furniture, and equipment used for its operation and maintenance.

## HOW DO I KNOW HOW MUCH BOAT INSURANCE I NEED?

In most cases you would insure the boat for the purchase price. Of course, if you got a really good deal on your boat and paid less than what the boat was worth, you would adjust your figure. Your best bet is to consult a boat dealer or marina and have a replacement cost appraisal done on the boat so that you can determine its true value.

## DOES IT MAKE A DIFFERENCE WHERE I OPERATE MY BOAT?

There are different rates charged for inland waters versus seacoast waters. Also, a shore river, like the Hudson River, differs from an inland lake, like Lake George in New York or Lake Meade in Nevada.

## DO I HAVE TO HAVE BOAT EXPERIENCE TO OBTAIN A BOAT POLICY?

Some insurance companies may require that you do have some boating experience. If you don't, the insurance company may suggest that you take a coast-guard or boating course in order to learn how to operate the boat.

## I DON'T HAVE A VERY GOOD AUTOMOBILE DRIVING RECORD. WILL THIS ALTER MY PREMIUM OR PREVENT ME FROM OBTAINING A BOAT POLICY?

Most insurance companies today find that a relationship exists between your automobile driving record and the manner in which you can be expected to operate a boat. Thus, if your driving record indicates convictions for DWI (driving while impaired) or speeding, you'll have a difficult time obtaining boat liability insurance.

## CAN I USE MY BOAT FOR WATERSKIING?

Most of the time the answer is yes. However, some insurance companies will ask you if you want to use the boat for waterskiing, and then take the option of refusing your insurance application.

## IS MY BOAT COVERED WHILE BEING CARRIED ON MY TRAILER?

Your boat is covered in and out of the water. The trailer itself is covered under your automobile policy.

## IS MY BOAT COVERED WHILE IN DRY DOCK?

Again, it is covered both in and out of the water.

## DOES IT MATTER WHERE I KEEP MY BOAT—AT A MARINA, OR AT MY HOUSE ON THE LAKE?

Generally it does not make a difference where you keep your boat; however, the insurance company does require you to notify them where it is being kept or moored.

## CAN I ALLOW OTHER PEOPLE TO OPERATE MY BOAT?

Just as with automobile insurance, any person you feel is capable of operating the boat responsibly is allowed to do so.

## IS MY PERSONAL PROPERTY COVERED UNDER THE BOAT POLICY?

Personal property, meaning clothing and items of that nature, are covered under your homeowners policy, if you have off-premises coverage.

## IS MY BOAT EQUIPMENT COVERED?

Yes, your policy will cover boat equipment such as radar detector, depth finder, bilge pump, your anchor, etc.

## IS THERE DIFFERENCE IN THE PREMIUM I'LL PAY IF I HAVE A SAILBOAT OR A MOTORBOAT?

In most cases the premium for a sailboat is much lower than for a motorboat. Your insurance company will want to know what type of motor you have, how fast the boat will go, the miles per hour, the horsepower, and the year, make, and model of the boat itself in order to determine the amount of your premiums.

## WHAT DOES THE LIABILITY PORTION OF MY BOAT INSURANCE COVER?

The liability section will provide for bodily injury to any persons on the boat who are injured. It also provides for injury to any persons in another boat, if you are in a collision and you are responsible for the accident.

## I'VE DECIDED TO HAVE A PARTY ON MY BOAT AND I'VE HIRED A CAPTAIN TO OPERATE THE BOAT WHILE WE SAIL AROUND THE BAY. AM I COVERED WHILE THE CAPTAIN IS OPERATING THE BOAT AND I AM PAYING HIM A FEE?

In most cases if this is an incidental type of exposure (you have hired him for this one occasion, not as a permanent employee) you would be covered. However, your best bet is to check your policy or ask your agent.

## IS THERE A LAY-UP PERIOD IN A BOAT POLICY?

A "lay-up" period is the time the boat is out of use. It may be in storage or secured to a dock. In the Northeast, the lay-up period is generally between October 1 and April 1. If you operate your boat during this period, you are not covered. The lay-up period varies depending upon your geographic location; Florida, for instance, has none.

# HOMEOWNERS INSURANCE

## THE BASICS

## WHAT IS A HOMEOWNERS POLICY AND HOW DOES IT PROTECT ME?

A homeowners policy is insurance coverage for your residence(s) and your personal property—where you live and what you own. Homeowners insurance is divided into two sections: property and personal liability.

Property coverage includes dwelling (the actual building in which you live), other structures (detached garage, barn, shed, etc.), personal property (furniture, clothing,

TV, VCR, etc.), and loss of use (if your home becomes uninhabitable due to fire, flood, etc.).

Personal liability means that if a claim or lawsuit is brought against you under the policy, the insurance company will represent you and pay any damages for which you are legally responsible.

## IS THERE A DEDUCTIBLE ON MY POLICY?

All homeowner, co-op, condo, and tenant (renter's) policies contain a deductible. The minimum deductible is usually $100, but may run as high as $10,000. Most insurance companies require a deductible of at least $250 or $500.

## HOW MUCH OF A DEDUCTIBLE SHOULD I BE LOOKING FOR WHEN I PURCHASE PROPERTY INSURANCE?

You should buy the highest deductible you can afford. If you can afford to pay for any damages under $1,000 out of your own pocket, take the $1,000 deductible. The higher the deductible, the lower your premiums.

## WHAT ARE THE DIFFERENT TYPES OF HOMEOWNER POLICIES AVAILABLE?

There are many different types of homeowner policies available. HO1, HO2, HO3, and HO5 are for people who own their homes. HO4 is for renters, HO6 is for condominium owners, and HO9 is for cooperatives. Some states have an HO8 for older homes.

An HO1 is the least common type of policy because of its very limited coverage. These policies cover you against fire, windstorm, civil commotion, smoke, hail, vehicular damage, explosion, riot, vandalism and malicious mischief, damage caused by burglars (but not the actual theft of your property), personal liability, and medical payments to others.

An HO2 provides broader-named-peril (see question below) coverage than the HO1. An HO3 is the most common due to its "all risk" (see below) coverage on the dwelling and broad coverage on the contents.

An HO5 is the top-of-the-line policy providing all-risk coverage on your house and contents. It's also the most expensive.

An HO4 is for renters who aren't concerned with insuring the building in which they live. It offers broad coverage on the contents, along with liability and medical payments.

Condominium owners need an HO6, which provides coverage on their contents as well as any improvements they may have made to their condo. The HO9 is similar to an HO6, but the coverages are directed to the cooperative owners.

Finally, some companies offer an HO8 for older homes with intrinsic values that can't be replaced today—such as an old Victorian home with plaster walls and fancy and extensive wood moldings.

## WHAT IS NAMED-PERIL COVERAGE?

Named-peril coverage means you are covered for the perils listed in the policy. Generally a named-peril-homeowner policy will cover the following items: fire, lightning and explosion, riot, windstorm or hail, aircraft, vehicles, sudden and accidental damage from smoke, vandalism, theft, falling objects, weight of ice, snow, or sleet, collapse of a building or part of a building, accidental discharge or overflow of water or steam, sudden and accidental cracking, burning, bulging, or tearing apart, freezing, and power surge.

Exactly what is covered depends on the insurance company and the particular policy. Some policies cover more items than are listed above, some cover less.

## WHAT IS AN ALL-RISK POLICY OR COVERAGE?

All risks means you are covered for all risks of loss, or just about any conceivable damage to your property, except for the listed exclusions (things that are not covered under the policy).

## WHAT IS NOT COVERED UNDER ALL RISK?

The following is a list of typical exclusions:

- Gradual loss: for instance, a loss caused by wear and tear or gradual deterioration by rust, mold, rot, warping, insects, and vermin.
- Contamination: for instance, a house served by a well finds its water supply contaminated by a leaking gas tank or industrial pollution.
- Loss by animals: damage to your home caused by animals, for example, a hole in the roof caused by squirrels (although the damage caused by rain coming through the hole would be covered).
- Escaping water: if a household appliance, swimming pool, plumbing, heating, or air-conditioning system breaks and causes loss, the loss caused by the water is covered; however, the appliance itself is not.
- Freezing water: companies do not pay for damage caused by water freezing in pipes if the building is vacant or unoccupied unless reasonable care was used to maintain heat in the home or the water was shut off and the plumbing drained.

- Surface water: for instance, a heavy rainstorm causes rising water that floods your basement. That is not covered.
- Ground water: meaning water that leaks or seeps through the ground into your home.
- Power interruption: food spoilage caused by the power interruption due to a brownout or a blackout.
- Structural movement: settling, cracking, shrinking, bulging, or expansion of pavement, patios, foundations, walls, floors, roofs, or ceilings.
- Water damage of outside structures: freezing, thawing, or the pressure of weight or water or ice affecting a fence, pavement, patio, swimming pool, hot tub, foundation, retaining wall, bulkhead, pier, wharf, dock, or bridge.
- Earthquake and earth movement.
- Neglect: any loss caused by your failure to use all reasonable means to protect your property, or any losses caused by negligent acts, errors by you or any other person in planning, construction, or maintenance.
- Intentional loss: any loss caused intentionally by you.
- Acts of war, and nuclear and radiation hazards.

## CAN I OBTAIN COVERAGE FOR ANY OF THESE EXCLUSIONS?

In California and other states where earthquakes are prevalent, you can usually obtain earthquake insurance. You cannot obtain coverage for the other exclusions.

## DOES NAMED PERIL ALSO HAVE EXCLUSIONS?

Yes, there are exclusions in all types of insurance policies. All of the exclusions listed above are also excluded in named-peril policies.

## IF I HAVE A CLAIM UNDER MY HOMEOWNERS POLICY, HOW LONG WILL IT TAKE BEFORE I GET MY MONEY?

It all depends on the type of claim and the particular insurance company—but it also depends on how prepared you are beforehand.

Suppose your house was broken into, and a lot of your property was stolen. The insurance company will require a written statement about what happened. They will also require a detailed list of what was stolen, the date you purchased these items, and the purchase amounts. They will also want purchase receipts for any highly valued items, such as your television set or VCR. You then submit all paperwork to the company.

If you have kept your receipts and know where they all are, it should not take you long to complete the paperwork. If your receipts are in no particular order in shoe boxes somewhere in your attic (or is it the basement?), filling out the forms can take you a while. The claim cannot be processed before you fill in the forms, however, so this part of the process depends on you.

With proper documentation, the check should be in your hands within a maximum of ten to fifteen working days.

## WHAT HAPPENS IF I DON'T HAVE RECEIPTS?

You're not expected to have receipts for everything. The more valuable the item, the more documentation the insurance company will demand. Keep receipts, credit-card slips, canceled checks; write down brands, models, and serial numbers of TVs, stereos, cameras, guns, etc. The burden of proof is upon you to prove to the company what you owned at the time of your claim. The company should not be expected to pay a claim on your say-so.

Insurance-department regulations in many states insist upon receipts before a company can pay a claim.

Proving a loss is often difficult. A formal inventory, listing what you own, its condition and value is best. Original receipts will also help establish your claim. If you have neither, look for old photographs—for instance, from a recent party at your home—to help you document your property. Finally, the company may accept affidavits from friends and neighbors.

Your best bet is to keep receipts, take pictures, keep a written record, have an appraisal done, and/or videotape everything.

## IF I HAVE A LARGE CLAIM—FOR INSTANCE, IF MY HOUSE IS TOTALLY DESTROYED—WILL MY INSURANCE POLICY BE CANCELED MIDTERM, OR NOT RENEWED WHEN MY TERM IS UP?

The provisions of most insurance policies do not permit the company to cancel midterm for losses. You should check with the rules and regulations in your state.

One large claim usually does not trigger a cancellation notice. But the circumstances surrounding that claim might. For instance, if you had large amounts of unprotected jewelry and fine arts and the insurance company wasn't aware of it, or if your premises were not protected properly and you had a large burglary, the insurance company might cancel your coverage.

In some cases the insurance company might feel that your claim is excessive and that you haven't been entirely truthful in submitting your bills or estimates. In that case they may pay the claim, but only after they receive proper documentation. Any hint of fraud or untruthfulness may result in an investigation.

A poor claims history will make any reputable company think twice before insuring you. Insurance is a business. If they feel they can't make money insuring you, they'll cancel or nonrenew your policy (where allowed by law).

## PROPERTY COVERAGE

## DWELLING

### WHAT IS DWELLING COVERAGE?

Dwelling coverage is the part of the policy that covers the actual structure in which you live. For example, during an electrical rainstorm, lightning hits the house, causes damage to your roof, and knocks out your alarm system. You would be paid to fix your roof and repair your alarm system and for any resulting water-damage loss.

Or suppose a leak in the shower pan in the upstairs bathroom causes water damage to the floor in the bathroom and the ceiling and a wall in the room downstairs. The entire floor in the bathroom has to be replaced, along with a new ceiling, new plasterboard, and a paint job downstairs. All this damage is covered by the dwelling portion of your policy.

### HOW MUCH DWELLING COVERAGE DO I NEED?

If your home is damaged so severely that you can no longer live in it, you want to be sure that your insurance will pay you to purchase or rebuild another home.

### HOW CAN I GUARANTEE THAT I WILL RECEIVE THE REPLACEMENT COST OF MY HOME?

There is an endorsement (an addition to a standard policy) that is added on to homeowner policies called a guaranteed replacement cost, dwelling replacement cost, or dwelling replacement cost extension.

When you obtain an insurance policy, you fill out a form to determine the cost of replacing your home (see next question). Suppose it is determined that it would cost $200,000 to replace your home. That's how much dwelling coverage you would obtain; then you would add the replacement cost endorsement.

One year goes by. Unfortunately, your house burns to the ground. Now, due to inflation and the rising costs of building supplies, it will take $230,000 to rebuild your house. Because you have the replacement cost endorsement, the insurance company will pay you $230,000 instead of the original $200,000 estimate.

At the time of loss, they will adjust the dwelling coverage to the $230,000, then bill you for the additional premium. The cost of the additional premium is well worth the $30,000 difference they have paid you. Most homeowner policies include a replacement cost endorsement; you shouldn't have a policy without it.

## HOW IS THE REPLACEMENT COST DETERMINED?

The replacement cost is determined by a form the insurance company supplies that is usually called the costimator or home evaluator. This form asks you many questions, such as how many bedrooms are in your home, how many bathrooms, is there a family room, a dining room, a kitchen? Is there a brick exterior, are there fireplaces, is there a breakfast nook, a walk-in closet? It also asks you the square footage of the house and what kinds of additional features you might have in the home, such as alarm systems, central air-conditioning, garbage disposals, or intercom. The insurance agent adds in factors such as local labor costs (plumbers, masons, carpenters, etc.) and the cost of materials in your area, and comes up with the replacement cost for your home.

On highly valued homes, some insurance companies come out and appraise the homes themselves. They use an industry-wide book that helps determine the replacement cost in your area. In the Northeast, where labor and material costs are highest, replacement costs range between $100 to $150 per square foot.

## WHAT ELSE DOES DWELLING COVERAGE INCLUDE?

An additional feature of the homeowners policy is that landscaping is covered. Most policies will cover trees, shrubs, plants, and lawns against certain kinds of losses, including fire, lightning, explosion, civil disturbance, vandalism, malicious mischief, theft, and loss caused by a vehicle.

For an example, an out-of-control car goes off the road in front of your house and hits the $1,000 tree that you just purchased. The cost of that tree would be covered. However, in most cases the coverage itself is limited to 5 percent of your dwelling coverage and not more than $1,000 for any one tree, shrub, or plant.

Another coverage that is automatically provided is fire-department charges. If a fire department is called to your house to protect it, and you are required to pay that fire department, the policy will pay usually up to $500. (Fire-department charges are still levied in some rural areas, although they are quickly disappearing. There is no provision in a homeowners policy to increase the $500 limit, although some companies will pay more.)

Lock replacement is also covered. If the keys to your home are lost or stolen, the homeowners policy will pay you for the costs of replacing the locks. There is usually a declaration that you must notify the insurance company in writing within seventy-two hours of losing the keys.

## OTHER STRUCTURES

# WHAT IS OTHER-STRUCTURES COVERAGE?

This portion of the policy covers any structures that are not attached to the home and are separated from the dwelling by clear space, for instance, a detached garage, a barn, a shed, a swimming pool, or tennis courts. This coverage is automatically included on all homeowner policies.

The coverage limit is 10 percent of what you carry on the dwelling. So if you have a $200,000 dwelling coverage, $20,000 is automatically provided for other structures.

## PERSONAL PROPERTY

# WHAT IS PERSONAL-PROPERTY COVERAGE?

Personal-property coverage covers all the contents located inside your home, including clothing, furniture, television, stereo, dishes, books, silverware, and small appliances such as toasters, blenders, and can openers. Large appliances are also considered personal property, including washing machines and dryers—anything that is in the house that you could take with you if you moved.

An example of personal-property coverage would be: Your washing machine overflows and causes extensive damage throughout your finished basement. The carpeting, couch, and end tables are ruined and must be replaced. The washing machine is not covered (it overflowed, it wasn't damaged); however, the ensuing damage caused by the overflow is covered.

Your oil burner has a puffback that causes soot damage to all the furniture and clothing in your bedroom. Again the oil-burner malfunction is not covered; however, the resulting damage is. In most cases the insurance company will ask you to try to clean the clothes and the furniture. If you cannot get the smell and soot out, the insurance company will allow you to purchase new items.

## HOW MUCH PERSONAL-PROPERTY COVERAGE CAN I GET?

The personal-property coverage amount is normally 50 percent of the dwelling amount. So a $200,000 dwelling policy would give you $100,000 of personal-property coverage. Some homeowner policies go as high as 70 percent.

## HOW DO I MAKE SURE I HAVE ENOUGH PERSONAL-PROPERTY COVERAGE?

Your agent can supply you with a home inventory booklet in which you describe each room in your house and its contents. You are told to provide the purchase date and price of each item listed. If you keep such an inventory, and you do have a claim, it's much easier to determine what was lost and what it would cost you to replace it.

A smart idea is to videotape your entire premises. The videotape should be kept off premises or in a vault in case you have a fire or your house is destroyed.

## IF I DO NEED TO REPLACE AN ITEM, HOW CAN I GUARANTEE THAT I'LL BE PAID AT TODAY'S PRICES, WITHOUT DEDUCTION FOR DEPRECIATION?

You can obtain a personal-property replacement cost endorsement. This endorsement works under the same principle as the dwelling replacement cost endorsement.

For example, suppose you have a five-year-old television set that is stolen or damaged. It originally cost you $300. The same-quality set might cost you $600 today. With the replacement cost endorsement, the insurance company will pay you the $600. Replacement cost coverage usually adds about 10 percent to your homeowners premium.

## IS MY PERSONAL PROPERTY COVERED AWAY FROM MY HOME?

Yes, with an endorsement called off-premises coverage. This covers your personal property while you are away from your premises. In other words, if your suitcase is stolen while you're on vacation, its contents would be covered under this portion of your policy. For an additional premium, the insurance company will cover 10 percent of your personal-property limit away from home.

## I HAVE A SECONDARY RESIDENCE AT THE BEACH. IS MY PERSONAL PROPERTY COVERED THERE AS WELL?

Yes, within that 10-percent limit.

## ARE MY CHILDREN'S PROPERTY COVERED WHEN THEY'RE AWAY AT COLLEGE?

As long as you have that 10-percent off-premises coverage, the answer is yes. However, some homeowner policies state that the child has to reside on campus in order for his property to be covered; they consider that a student living in an apartment off campus for nine to ten months is really in a separate residence.

## WHAT IF I HAVE HIGHLY VALUABLE PERSONAL PROPERTY, SUCH AS JEWELRY, FURS, OR FINE ARTS? DOES MY POLICY HAVE CERTAIN LIMITATIONS?

All homeowner policies have special limits of liability on certain types of property, usually jewelry, furs, silver, fine arts, stamps, guns, and cash. The actual coverage limits vary from policy to policy. The most common limit for cash is $100; however, it can go up to $1,000 depending upon the insurance company and the type of policy. Jewelry, furs, silver, stamps, and most other types of property are usually limited to anywhere between $1,000 and $5,000.

## WHAT DO I DO IF MY PROPERTY EXCEEDS THOSE VALUES?

You would then add scheduled personal-property coverage to your homeowner policy. This is also known as valuable-articles coverage or valuable-items coverage, or a personal-article floater. By doing so, you specifically list and agree on amount of coverage for each valuable item.

For example, a jewelry schedule would list one fourteen-karat yellow-gold diamond engagement ring, valued at $3,000. Then you might have a fourteen-karat yellow-gold tennis bracelet for $2,000. You would also schedule your furs, silver, artworks, or any other valuables that also exceed your policy's limits.

## IS THE VALUE LISTED ON MY "SCHEDULE" WHAT I'LL RECEIVE FROM THE INSURANCE COMPANY IN CASE OF A LOSS?

The value listed on the schedule becomes the maximum limit the company will pay for that item. Some companies use the limit as an "agreed value"—that means you'll receive just what it's insured for in the event of a loss. Some companies stipulate that should they be able to obtain a duplicate for less, they will pay the lower amount.

## HOW DO I APPLY FOR VALUABLE-ARTICLE COVERAGE?

Your agent will supply you with an application. You complete the application and return it, along with an appraisal or bill of sale for each item that is listed. The appraisals or bills of sale usually cannot be more than three years old or the insurance companies will not accept them.

## WHAT AM I COVERED FOR UNDER A FLOATER POLICY?

A floater policy is "all risk," meaning you're covered for all risks of loss, including loss, theft, and damage. If a painting falls off the wall and cracks, or a bronze sculpture falls off its stand and breaks—you're covered. If a child colors in your Picasso, or your dog eats your stamp collection—you're covered. You're also covered if the diamond in your ring falls out and is lost, or if your Rolex is stolen. As long as the particular item is listed in the policy, it is covered for almost any possible type of loss or damage.

## HOW IS A PREMIUM DETERMINED ON A FLOATER POLICY?

There is a determined rate per $100 of coverage. For instance, jewelry is usually $2 per $100 of coverage. That means that if you insure a ring worth $3,000, it will cost you $60 in premiums.

There are certain types of policy provisions that state if you have a very large schedule, meaning $100,000 or more, these published rates do not apply, and the insurance company will determine how much you'll have to pay.

## WHAT TYPES OF ARTICLES ARE ELIGIBLE FOR VALUABLE-ARTICLES POLICY?

Jewelry, furs, fine arts (paintings, etchings, pictures, tapestries, art-glass windows); rare books, statues, antiques, manuscripts, porcelain, and rare glass; silverware, including sterling silver, gold, or pewter; plated ware, tableware, trays, trophies, and similar household articles; stamps and coins; musical instruments; cameras, projection machines, films, and related equipment; and items of historical value or artistic merit.

## HOW DO I KNOW THAT MY ITEMS ARE STILL INSURED PROPERLY FIVE YEARS AFTER A POLICY IS WRITTEN?

It is recommended that every few years you obtain new appraisals on all scheduled items. This will determine that you are insured to current value on items that have appreciated as well as depreciated. Your schedule can then be adjusted accordingly.

## ARE MY PAINTINGS COVERED IF I PUT THEM ON DISPLAY?

It depends on where they are to be displayed. If you put them on exhibition at a fairgrounds or on the premises of a national or international exposition, they are not covered. If you put them on display at a museum or an auction house, however, they are covered.

## IS MY JEWELRY COVERED IF I LOAN IT TO MY CHILDREN OR FRIENDS?

Yes. You have coverage if you give your jewelry to your children or friends to wear from time to time.

## MY STERLING SILVER IS TARNISHED AND IT CANNOT BE REPAIRED, AM I COVERED FOR THIS?

No. An exclusion in the policy states that no loss caused by wear and tear, gradual deterioration, rust, mold, rot, warping, insects or vermin is covered.

## WHAT IS A PUBLIC ADJUSTER AND SHOULD I HIRE ONE?

A public adjuster represents you, for a fee, to assist you in collecting a claim from your insurance company. If you are with a reliable, high-quality insurance company, and have a minor loss, a public adjuster is not necessary. For instance, if you lost an expensive watch, it's an easy claim to handle. However, if you have fire damage to your home and don't have a record of what you lost, it might be to your advantage to hire a public adjuster—especially if you're concerned about the quality of your insurance company.

## HOW MUCH WOULD I HAVE TO PAY A PUBLIC ADJUSTER?

Be prepared to pay between 5 and 15 percent of what you obtain from the insurance company for the services of the public adjuster. A public adjuster should be licensed by the state and be bonded, which means you would have some recourse if he gets your claim check and disappears with it.

## HOW DO I KNOW WHEN TO USE A PUBLIC ADJUSTER?

Insurance agents recognize the need for public adjusters on certain complex claims. If you are with a quality insurance company and have good documentation of the items you've lost, you shouldn't need a public adjuster. Discuss the situation with your agent; he will be able to let you know whether he thinks it necessary that you hire somebody.

## LOSS OF USE

## WHAT IS LOSS-OF-USE COVERAGE?

If your home becomes uninhabitable due to a covered loss (fire, water damage, etc.), loss-of-use coverage would apply for any increase in your living expenses in order to maintain your normal standard of living.

In other words, if your house is destroyed, loss of use will cover your living expenses for the reasonable amount of time it takes to repair or rebuild your house.

In most cases, coverage is limited to 20 percent of your dwelling coverage. However, some policies allow for an unlimited amount of coverage.

## IT'S SATURDAY NIGHT, AND I'VE JUST HAD A TERRIBLE FLOOD IN MY HOUSE—SO BAD THAT I CAN'T STAY THE NIGHT. MY AGENT ISN'T IN AND THE INSURANCE COMPANY IS CLOSED. WHAT DO I DO?

First, protect your home and its contents from any further damage. If your premises are open and accessible and there are contents of your home that haven't been damaged by the flood, you have authority under your policy to move your property to a safe place by hiring someone to move it, by moving it to a warehouse, or by storing it at a friend's house. This cost of protecting your property would be a covered item under the claim.

As soon as possible, notify your insurance agent or company. Indicate that you had an extensive loss, that your home or apartment is uninhabitable, and that you've moved to a hotel or motel temporarily. The provisions of most homeowners policies or tenants policies will enable you to live in a hotel or motel until your regular residence has been repaired. You will be reimbursed for the difference between your normal living expenses and the additional expenses being incurred by living outside of the house.

## NOW THAT I AM LIVING IN A HOTEL OR MOTEL, I HAVE TO EAT OUT. ARE THOSE COSTS COVERED?

The company will usually reimburse you the difference between your normal grocery bills and the cost to eat out. Keep in mind you must be reasonable and stay within your normal life-style. The insurance company will not pay for you to dine at the best four-star restaurants each night if that is something you would not normally do.

## MY HOME AND ALL ITS CONTENTS WERE DESTROYED IN A FIRE. I HAVE TO BUY NEW CLOTHES TO GO TO WORK, AND I HAVE TO PAY FOR THE HOTEL. I DON'T HAVE MUCH MONEY TO LAY OUT FOR THESE THINGS. WHAT CAN I DO?

If you are insured with a reliable insurance company, you may be able to get an advance on your claim. For instance, a friend's house was destroyed by a gas explosion. The house was totally destroyed, along with everything my friends owned. Within one week, they were able to get a $25,000 advance so that they could rent temporary living quarters, purchase replacement clothing, and resume their normal life. The advance helped them get through a difficult time, and survive until the entire insurance settlement was received.

## I HAVE A TWO-FAMILY HOME. I LIVE IN ONE HALF AND I RENT OUT THE OTHER HALF. IF THIS HOME IS DESTROYED, WILL I BE COMPENSATED FOR THE RENT I'M GOING TO LOSE?

If the part of your house you generally rent out to others is uninhabitable due to a covered loss, the insurance company will cover its fair rental value, up to the 20-percent limit of the policy.

Let's say your home is insured for $250,000. You would have 20 percent, or $50,000, to pay for the loss of the fair rental value of the house. The company would pay until the damage could be repaired or the claim is settled.

## PERSONAL LIABILITY

## WHAT IS PERSONAL LIABILITY COVERAGE?

If a claim or lawsuit is brought against you under your homeowners policy, the insurance company will represent you and pay any damages for which you are legally responsible. Personal liability claims may be brought for personal injury, as well as for libel, slander, defamation of character, and invasion of privacy.

## WHAT DOES BODILY INJURY MEAN?

It includes physical bodily harm, shock, and mental anguish, including sickness or disease that results from the injury and required care for it, loss of services, and resulting death.

## HOW MUCH PERSONAL LIABILITY COVERAGE SHOULD I HAVE?

The least amount of coverage you can get today is $50,000, and the highest is $1,000,000. However, the premium difference between a $100,000 policy and a $1,000,000 policy may be as little as $30 to $40 a year, so it is usually worth it to purchase as much coverage as possible.

## OUR DAUGHTER HAS A PARTY, AND WHILE ONE OF HER FRIENDS IS AT OUR HOME, SHE FALLS AND NEEDS MEDICAL ATTENTION. AM I COVERED FOR THIS?

Yes. Your personal liability would provide payment for her medical bills.

## MY SON HAS A FIGHT WITH ANOTHER BOY AND CALLS HIM ALL KINDS OF NAMES AND REALLY EMBARRASSES HIM. A LAWSUIT IS BROUGHT AGAINST HIM FOR DEFAMATION OF CHARACTER. AM I COVERED FOR THIS?

Yes, the personal liability coverage under your policy would then apply. Some insurance companies charge extra for adding personal injury coverage, which refers to libel, slander, defamation of character, wrongful eviction, etc.

## DURING A WINDSTORM, ONE OF THE TREES ON MY PROPERTY FALLS AND HITS THE HOUSE NEXT DOOR. AM I COVERED FOR THIS?

Your personal liability coverage also covers property damage, meaning physical injury or destruction of tangible property. Your neighbor would then be paid to repair the portion of his house that was damaged.

## A GUEST WHO STAYED IN MY HOME FOR A FEW WEEKS FOUND THAT HIS CLOTHING WAS DESTROYED BY MY FIVE-YEAR-OLD-SON. IS THERE COVERAGE FOR THIS?

Most homeowner policies will cover property of others, generally up to a $1,000 limit. This property must be damaged or destroyed by a covered person (you or a family member). This does not, however, pertain to property owned by or rented to a tenant or a resident in your household.

## MY POCKETBOOK WAS STOLEN AND MY CREDIT CARDS WERE ILLEGALLY USED BY THE THIEF. AM I COVERED FOR THIS?

Yes. Most homeowner policies will cover a person's legal obligation up to a total limit of $10,000 for loss or theft of credit or bank card, issued in your name or the name of a family member, as well as loss caused by forgery or alteration of a check.

## I HAVE A HOUSEKEEPER WHO WORKS FOR ME FORTY HOURS A WEEK. AM I COVERED IF SHE GETS HURT ON MY PROPERTY?

Your personal liability coverage only applies to employees in your residence if they work for you fewer than forty hours a week. If you employ someone for forty hours or more, you must obtain a workers' compensation policy.

If you have an employee who works for you less than forty hours a week, or if you have a baby-sitter or gardener or a housecleaner who comes in once a week, they will be covered for medical bills or injuries if they are hurt on your premises. The common limit for this coverage is $100,000.

Workers' compensation is mandatory coverage under your homeowners policy in many states. However, it generally provides limited coverage for those working forty hours or less. This should be thoroughly reviewed with your agent.

## I MAINTAIN AN OFFICE IN MY HOME AND I MAY HAVE PEOPLE COMING IN AND OUT OF THE HOME ONCE OR TWICE A WEEK. AM I COVERED?

Most homeowner policies exclude any business pursuits. However, some insurance companies offer what is called incidental business or office liability. Depending upon what type of business you're in, you may be able to add this coverage for an additional premium.

## I OWN A SMALL SAILBOAT THAT I USE MAYBE FOUR OR FIVE TIMES A YEAR. AM I COVERED FOR LIABILITY ON THIS?

The answer to this question depends on the actual insurance policy. Some policies will cover watercraft under the liability section of your policy if the craft are under nineteen feet and do not go over twenty to twenty-five miles per hour. If your boat is not covered under the homeowner policy, then you must obtain a separate boat policy.

## I AM ON THE BOARD OF DIRECTORS OF MY COUNTRY CLUB. AM I COVERED FOR ANY LIABILITY ARISING OUT OF MY ACTIONS AS A MEMBER OF THE BOARD?

Homeowner policies exclude coverage for anyone while serving on the board of a for-profit corporation. While some companies cover board members of nonprofit organizations, your best bet is to be sure the organization has a directors' and officers' liability policy in force that covers you. This is very important since board members can be held personally liable.

## UMBRELLA INSURANCE

### WHAT IS AN UMBRELLA POLICY?

Umbrella insurance is also known as personal excess insurance, or personal catastrophes policies. Whatever it is called, it provides additional liability coverage over the limits contained on your auto, homeowner, co-op, condo, watercraft, or tenant policy. Policies are written in increments of $1,000,000 and usually contain a $250 deductible.

### WHY SHOULD I HAVE A POLICY SUCH AS THIS?

In today's society lawsuits are very common. If you are found legally liable to pay damages to a claimant, and if the claim exceeds the liability limits of your insurance, you are responsible to pay the difference.

Suppose your homeowner policy includes a $100,000 personal liability coverage, and you also have a $1,000,000 umbrella policy. While a guest is at your home, she trips over TV wire and sustains head injuries and a broken shoulder. The guest requires hospitalization and extensive therapy to regain the use of her shoulder. If your guest's medical bills exceed $100,000, your umbrella insurance would then come into play. In addition, if the guest brought a lawsuit against you for her pain and suffering, you would also be covered.

Or, suppose your auto-policy coverage is $250,000 per person, with a $500,000-per-accident liability limit. You also maintain a $3,000,000 umbrella policy. While carpooling four children to school, you lose control of your vehicle and you run off the road into a tree. Everyone in the vehicle is hurt. Some require hospitalization and some are treated and released from the emergency room. Your auto policy will provide bodily injury coverage for up to $250,000 per person; however, it has a $500,000 limit per occurrence. Your personal-excess-liability policy would then come into play after the auto-policy limits were exhausted.

## IF I AM SUED BY SOMEBODY, DO I HAVE TO GET MY OWN LAWYER?

Not necessarily. The insurance company will provide an attorney to defend you against a suit if there is coverage under your policy. Any judgments against you would be paid by the insurance company up to the limit of the liability policy.

There are times when you might want to consult your own attorney to work with the insurance company. For example, suppose you carry homeowner liability limits of $300,000 and you also have a personal umbrella policy with $1,000,000 limits. Your lawn mower kicks up a stone and blinds a passerby who then brings suit against you for his injuries. The suit may ask for a judgment of $3,000,000, which is in excess of your combined homeowner and umbrella liability limits. Your policies only provide a total of $1,300,000 coverage and you can be held personally liable for any judgments in excess of that amount. In such a case you might want to have your attorney contact the insurance company.

## HOW MUCH UMBRELLA INSURANCE SHOULD I CARRY?

To determine how much umbrella insurance that you need, you should evaluate your personal assets. You should also evaluate your personal exposures, or circumstances under which you might be sued. If you have teenage children driving vehicles, if you are renting your home to others, or if you're involved in hazardous types of recreational activities, such as speedboating, you might want to carry more than the $1,000,000 standard policy. Usually you can buy up to $10,000,000 or $20,000,000 coverage. Again, if you do not have assets of that magnitude, stick with the smaller amounts of $1,000,000 or $2,000,000.

## WHAT ARE TYPICAL COSTS FOR UMBRELLA INSURANCE?

If you have an average homeowners policy and two vehicles, your premium for $1,000,000 coverage would be approximately $200 a year. If you have many more vehicles and several homes and teenage drivers, your premium could go up to $500 to $600 per million.

## I HAVE TWO TEENAGE CHILDREN, BOTH WITH BAD DRIVING RECORDS. WILL I STILL BE ABLE TO GET UMBRELLA COVERAGE?

Coverage is not available to everyone. Remember that this is a liability policy, and if the company feels the driving records indicate the likelihood of a large claim, they will decline to cover you. Excess and surplus markets—such as Lloyd's of London—will sometimes offer higher liability limits, albeit at increased premiums. Premiums can range between $500 to $1,500 per million for those in the high-risk categories.

# CO-OP, CONDO, AND TENANT INSURANCE

## WHAT IS COOPERATIVE AND CONDOMINIUM INSURANCE?

As a co-op or condo-unit owner, you either own shares in an association or you own the apartment itself. Condo and co-op policies are generally the same types of policies with different names. And like homeowners insurance, it's divided into two sections, the first being the property section and the second being the liability section. Liability coverage for co-ops and condos is the same as in a homeowners policy.

## HOW DO I INSURE MY CO-OP OR CONDO?

First of all you want to insure your personal property, meaning your clothing, furniture, stereo, television, dishes, appliances, silverware, books, photo albums, records, anything you can take with you if you walk out. Most of this coverage is the same as it is for homeowners.

## HOW DO I KNOW HOW MUCH PERSONAL-PROPERTY INSURANCE I NEED?

You use the same home inventory booklet as you would for a homeowners policy (which you can obtain from your agent). The booklet suggests you go from room to room in your apartment or town house and list all the items in each room, when you purchased them, and the purchase price. Once you have completed this booklet, your agent can help you determine how much coverage you need.

## IS THERE A MINIMUM AMOUNT OF PERSONAL-PROPERTY COVERAGE?

Most insurance companies today require a minimum personal-property or contents limit of $15,000 to $20,000.

## I PURCHASED MY CONDO FOR $200,000. SHOULD I INSURE IT FOR THAT AMOUNT?

You do not have to insure a co-op or condo for the purchase price. The co-op or condo association will have a master insurance policy that provides coverage for the actual structure or the building. If there is a total loss on the building, their insurance policy will pay to rebuild the building.

However, you are responsible for the inside of your apartment, such as the walls, floors, paneling, wallpaper, and parts of the plumbing and electrical systems, cabinets, glass mirrors, any custom molding or marble work that you have in the apartment. This coverage may be called additions, alterations, or improvements, depending on the company.

The responsibilities of the condominium or cooperative are spelled out in their bylaws, deed, or other governing documents. Check with your attorney or board of directors to be sure you fully understand what areas come under their jurisdiction and what areas are your responsibility.

## IF THERE IS A FIRE IN THE HALLWAY OF MY APARTMENT BUILDING, AND THE CO-OP OR CONDO ASSOCIATION ASSESSES EACH UNIT OWNER TO PAY FOR THE REPAIRS, CAN I PUT A CLAIM IN UNDER MY CO-OP OR CONDO POLICY?

The coverage that would apply here is called loss assessment. Some policies automatically provide coverage up to $1,000; however, some don't. There is an endorsement available to buy loss assessment coverage, usually up to a maximum of $50,000. Of course, there would be an additional premium for this coverage.

The co-op or condo association may have insurance to cover the loss. However, their policy could contain a $10,000 deductible. They may then assess you to pay for their deductible; again this coverage would apply under loss assessment.

## IS THERE LOSS-OF-USE COVERAGE FOR MY CONDO OR CO-OP?

Loss-of-use coverage for condos and co-ops is generally 20 percent of the personal-property limit. The coverage is the same as that for homeowners policies.

## WHAT IS TENANTS INSURANCE?

Tenants insurance is exactly the same as co-op and condo insurance with the exception of the additions-and-alterations coverage as well as the loss assessments. Again, the liability coverage is the same as a homeowners policy.

# COMMERCIAL PROPERTY AND BUSINESS INSURANCE

## THE BASICS

## I AM SIGNING A LEASE, AND PLAN TO OPEN MY NEW BUSINESS IN TWO MONTHS. WHEN DO I NEED TO START MY BUSINESS COVERAGE?

Your insurance coverage should begin with the effective date of your lease or the date you take possession of the premises—whichever comes first.

## I AM OPENING A BUSINESS AND SIGNING A COMMERCIAL LEASE. DOES THE LEASE INCLUDE INSURANCE REQUIREMENTS?

Most commercial leases require you to carry certain liability limits. The higher the liability limits called for in the lease, the higher your premiums will be. Leases generally request a minimum of $1,000,000 of liability coverage, but limits of $3,000,000 and even $5,000,000 are not uncommon today.

Commercial general liability policies normally offer limits of up to $1,000,000. To increase your coverage above this limit, you will need to purchase an umbrella or excess liability policy. Prices for umbrella or excess liability policies vary depending upon the type of company or business you have. A pet store may spend $300 per million for the excess coverage while a machine shop may spend $3,000 or more.

Ask both your insurance agent and your attorney to review your lease with you; they may be able to negotiate a reduction of the liability limits with the landlord.

## WHAT'S THE DIFFERENCE BETWEEN AN UMBRELLA LIABILITY POLICY AND AN EXCESS LIABILITY POLICY?

Both policies provide liability limits above what you have in your commercial general liability policy, and are usually issued in increments of $1,000,000. An umbrella policy will provide broader coverage than the general liability policy, while an excess policy simply extends the liability limits without broadening the coverage.

## WHAT OTHER INSURANCE REQUIREMENT MIGHT APPEAR IN THE LEASE?

A large number of leases today contain a "waiver of subrogation" clause, which basically states that should your negligence cause damage to the landlord's property, the landlord and his insurance company will be prohibited from seeking redress from you. A joint waiver of subrogation would prohibit either you or the landlord (or your insurance companies) from going after the other party.

Suppose, for example, you have made repeated complaints to the landlord regarding a sparking at one outlet in your office. The landlord has done nothing to correct the problem and one night there is a serious fire caused by the faulty outlet. Your insurance company would pay for your damages, the landlord's company would pay for the damages to the building. However, with a joint waiver, your insurance company would not be able to sue the landlord to recover the money paid to you.

Your landlord might also want to be named as an additional insured under your policy. Should a suit be brought against you and the landlord, the landlord could seek protection as an additional insured under your liability policy.

## IN MY LEASE, THE LANDLORD HAS REQUESTED THAT I SEND HIM A CERTIFICATE OF INSURANCE. WHAT IS IT AND DOES IT COST ME ANY MONEY?

A certificate of insurance is issued by your insurance agent or insurance company and is evidence that you have insurance coverage in force. There is generally no charge for this service. A certificate indicates your insurance company, policy number, dates of coverage, limits of liability, and any special conditions such as additional insureds.

## WHAT SHOULD I DO TO PREPARE MYSELF PRIOR TO DISCUSSING BUSINESS INSURANCE WITH AN AGENT OR AN INSURANCE COMPANY?

If you are opening a store or an office, you should know the square footage of the premises you're going to occupy. You should be prepared to answer numerous questions, such as: What are your estimated sales? What is your estimated payroll? How many and what type of employees will you be hiring? What type of product will you be selling, or what type of service will you be providing? Will you have cash on the premises? Are you susceptible to burglary—is the product you're selling easily disposed of on the street? What type of protection do you have? Do you have roll-down gates or an alarm system? Do you have a sprinkler system? All of this information is necessary for an agent to determine what type and how much insurance you need.

## PROPERTY INSURANCE

## HOW DO I KNOW WHAT KIND OF PROPERTY COVERAGE I NEED FOR MY BUSINESS?

Consider the nature of the property or the contents of your business, and also what you would like your coverage to include, i.e., fire, smoke damage, sprinkler leakage, water damage, burglary, robbery, flood—depending on your type of business. Water damage might be of major concern to an electronics retailer, but not so important to an umbrella store. In your type of business you might have cash on hand, and might be concerned about a holdup or cash robbery. You might also be concerned about employee fidelity or theft of merchandise by employees.

## I WAS TOLD I COULD CHOOSE TO HAVE MY CONTENTS INSURED AT ACTUAL CASH VALUE OR AT REPLACEMENT COSTS. WHY WOULDN'T I CHOOSE REPLACEMENT COSTS?

If you choose replacement costs as your method of reimbursement, the company is obligated to buy you new equipment, furniture, or stock at current price levels. However, there are several things to keep in mind. One, that in order for the provision to kick in, you must replace those items. Two, you may have some obsolete equipment or equipment that you have had for a number of years or equipment that you might have purchased used that you don't need to insure for full replacement cost. This equipment might not even be available today except on a resale market.

## IN OTHER WORDS, IF I TAKE THE REPLACEMENT COST OPTION, EVERYTHING THAT I AM INSURING HAS TO BE AT REPLACEMENT COST?

Usually, yes. Certain provisions of the replacement cost option might indicate that items over ten years old are not reimbursable at replacement cost. First read the provision for replacement costs in your policy and then determine whether you want to opt for this type of coverage.

## WHAT KIND OF CRITERIA WOULD I USE TO HELP ME DECIDE?

The best thing to do is a physical inventory, if that's practical. Separate your machinery, your furniture, your stock, and your improvements and betterments. If you're a new business and everything is brand new, you most probably want a replacement cost provision.

## DO INSURANCE COMPANIES DEPRECIATE AT THE SAME RATE MY ACCOUNTANT DEPRECIATES MY STOCK, EQUIPMENT, FURNITURE, AND FIXTURES?

Insurance companies usually have a depreciation table that lists various equipment values and how fast they might depreciate. This has no relationship to what the government allows under your tax forms.

## HOW DOES DEPRECIATION WORK?

Suppose you buy a new typewriter. The insurance company, by testing and determination, may indicate that the average typewriter has a five-year life span. If the typewriter was stolen after a year, under the actual-cash-value provision you would probably get 80 percent of the new value of that particular typewriter. After two and a half years, half the life is used, therefore it is worth only 50 percent.

Some items don't depreciate much at all; some depreciate faster than others. It is important that you review this with your insurance agent if you have valuable equipment or machinery that can only be replaced with new equipment.

## I RUN A SMALL COMPUTER REPAIR SERVICE. ARE MY CUSTOMERS' COMPUTERS COVERED WHILE THEY ARE ON MY PREMISES?

General liability policies exclude coverages for property of others in your care, custody, or control. There are various methods of covering this property that can be explained to you by your agent. Items left on your property for you to work on or repair would fall in this category.

## I HAVE SPENT $100,000 TO REARRANGE MY OFFICE SPACE, REMOVE WALLS, SET UP PERMANENT PARTITIONS, AND INSTALL NEW FLOORING. HOW WOULD I PROTECT MY INVESTMENT SHOULD I HAVE WATER DAMAGE OR FIRE?

Additions and alterations made to the premises you occupy are known as improvements and betterments. These improvements can range from several hundred to hundreds of thousands of dollars. If the premises are destroyed by fire, you want to make sure the costs of the improvements and betterments are covered.

You should notify your agent of the value of the permanent improvements you've installed, and ask him to revise your property insurance accordingly.

## WHAT ABOUT THE LOSS OF INCOME THAT I MIGHT SUSTAIN IF I SHOULD HAVE A MAJOR FIRE AND BE OUT OF BUSINESS FOR THREE OR FOUR MONTHS?

There is a type of insurance called business interruption coverage, which is available in many forms. One form might just pay for loss of earnings, another might include salaries for you and your key employees. Another form might include all of your ordinary payroll.

## WHAT IS EXTRA EXPENSE INSURANCE?

Extra expense insurance will pay your costs over your normal operating costs during a shutdown caused by a covered peril (fire, water damage, etc.). These additional expenses can enable you to resume business quickly.

Suppose your store had a major fire and won't be repaired for three to four months. You have several options. You can rent another store. Even if the rent is higher, the difference would be covered under extra expense. You can lease or purchase the necessary equipment to start again, and have that equipment shipped to you as quickly as possible. The purchase of the equipment would be covered under the property section of your policy; however, the costs to facilitate getting that equipment quickly would be covered under the extra expense portion of your policy, as would the hiring of temporary employees to get your business back in operation promptly.

## ARE THERE OTHER FORMS OF BUSINESS INTERRUPTION COVERAGES?

Suppose you own a small building and you rent out several stores to others. If you have a fire in that building, your tenants will not be paying rent. You could purchase a form of business interruption insurance called rental value. This would pay for your loss of rental income during a construction period.

## I'M OPENING A RETAIL BUSINESS ON THE GROUND FLOOR WITH A LARGE PLATE-GLASS WINDOW. WHO'S RESPONSIBLE FOR THE GLASS?

Many leases require that you be responsible for the glass. In many areas of the country this can be a major expense, so you may want to obtain plate-glass insurance. Also, be aware that if you have a sign or lettering on your glass window, you may have to pay an additional premium to cover the cost of redoing the lettering.

## I AM A DENTIST, AND ALL MY ACCOUNT RECORDS ARE IN MY OFFICE. IS THERE ANY INSURANCE TO COVER THE POSSIBLE LOSS OF THESE RECORDS?

If it would be difficult to determine who owes you money if your records were destroyed in a fire, you might want to discuss accounts receivable insurance. Accounts receivable insurance will assist you in collecting money due you due to loss of records.

Let's say you have a dental office that was damaged by fire and all your clients' billings were destroyed. If you have accounts receivables insurance, the insurance company would review your prior accounting records with you and discuss what your total accounts receivable was over the previous quarters. You'll deduct any payments that would normally come in for bills that were already sent to your clients. The balance of unpaid bills that would be unreconcilable would be paid under the accounts receivable insurance.

## WHAT ABOUT THE DENTAL RECORDS THAT WERE DESTROYED IN THE FIRE? CAN I BUY COVERAGE TO PROTECT ME FOR THE TIME THAT I NEED TO RECONSTRUCT MY FILES?

A normal insurance policy will just pay for the replacement of the file itself, not the work that was done to create that file. Reconstruction of files or records destroyed in a fire or by water damage, or stolen can be protected by coverage called valuable papers coverage. This type of coverage is usually sold to lawyers, insurance agents, doctors, dentists, architects, engineers, market research firms—those types of companies that have records that are valuable, irreplaceable, and one of a kind.

## HOW CAN I SAVE ON MY PROPERTY-INSURANCE COSTS?

In most cases, the installation of a central station alarm system will reduce your premiums. You can also consider taking higher deductibles.

Insurance companies will require certain businesses dealing with target theft items, such as cigarettes, liquor, furs, electronics, jewelry, etc., to have an alarm system before they provide any theft coverage. Your insurance agent can review the various types of alarm systems with you so the system you install will meet the insurance company's requirements.

## LIABILITY INSURANCE

## WHAT TYPE OF CASUALTY (LIABILITY) INSURANCE SHOULD I BUY?

Standard insurance for most small business is known as a comprehensive general liability policy, and it incorporates most of the endorsements you would need to run a small retail, wholesale, or service business.

## WHAT ARE SOME OF THE PROVISIONS OF A STANDARD GENERAL LIABILITY POLICY?

Standard provisions include limits for bodily injury to others, and damage to property of others. Usually there is a combined limit for both. For example, you would buy a policy covering $1,000,000 in damages both to bodily injury and property.

## WHAT ELSE WOULD BE COVERED UNDER THIS LIABILITY POLICY?

A broad-form comprehensive general liability policy can cover you for personal injury as well, which would include a suit brought against you for defamation of character or false arrest. Let's take an example where a man came into your store and you accused him of shoplifting. You called the police and had the man arrested. If it was later proven that this man was not shoplifting, he could sue you for false arrest. This would be a covered claim under your broad-form general liability endorsement.

## I REALIZE THAT AN ATTORNEY MAY BE NECESSARY IN CASE OF A CLAIM. HOW ARE THE LEGAL FEES HANDLED?

Most policies provide for legal fees outside the limit of liability. Thus, if you have a $1,000,000 liability policy and the suit against you results in a judgment of $1,000,000, the insurance company will pay the $1,000,000 judgment *and* will also pay for the legal fees incurred while defending you. Legal fees are often substantial and can easily amount to 30 percent or more of the judgment.

These legal fees cover the attorney retained by your insurance company to defend you. They will not cover any attorney you hire on your own.

## CAN I HIRE MY OWN ATTORNEY IF THERE IS A SUIT AGAINST ME?

Not usually. Most insurance companies require that their attorneys be used or that they assign an attorney to you. The only time that it would be advisable to hire your own attorney is if the suit is in excess of your policy limits.

In other words, if your policy is limited to coverage of $1,000,000 and you are sued for $2,000,000, you should immediately discuss the circumstances with and possibly retain your own attorney to defend you for the difference.

## HOW DOES THE $1,000,000 LIMIT APPLY? IS IT PER CLAIM, PER INDIVIDUAL, PER YEAR?

New policies normally cover $1,000,000 per claim. A second number will appear in your policy provisions that indicates an aggregate limit, or the most the insurance company will pay in one year. Generally, the aggregates are double the limits. For example, a policy might provide for $1,000,000 each occurrence with a $2,000,000 general aggregate.

## I SELL A PRODUCT TO THE PUBLIC. IS THERE ANY PROVISION IN MY POLICY TO COVER INJURIES CAUSED BY THOSE PRODUCTS?

The standard comprehensive general liability policy now includes coverage for products liability, which means bodily injury or property damage caused by your product.

For instance, if you sell children's wear and one of your garments catches on fire and injures a child, there could be a large products liability suit against you contending that the material was highly inflammable. This type of suit would be covered under your products liability.

Premiums for product liability are based upon rates that reflect the products you manufacture, distribute, or sell. Most rates are expressed per $1,000 of sales, although different rating bases are used for various industries. A company producing bolts used in the aircraft industry would have a much higher rate than that of an office supply store.

## WHAT HAPPENS IN THE ABOVE CASE ABOUT THE INFLAMMABLE MATERIAL IF I PURCHASED THE GARMENT FROM A MANUFACTURER AND MY COMPANY ONLY SOLD THE GARMENT?

Generally an attorney will sue everyone involved, from the manufacturer of the material used in the garment to the retail store that sold it. The courts will decide who is negligent. In the above example, the chances are that the fabric supplier and manufacturer will be held liable. You might still incur substantial defense costs that are covered under the products liability section of your liability policy.

Your insurance becomes particularly important if the fabric supplier is located out of the United States and/or the manufacturer has gone out of business. The court might then look to the "deepest pocket" to be sure the injured party is compensated.

## WHAT DOES THE "DEEPEST POCKET" MEAN?

The deepest pocket is the person with the most insurance, the most money or the most assets. Even though you might be liable for only a small percentage of the claim, you might be responsible for a larger percentage of the award because you have the most assets or most insurance.

## WHAT IF I HAVE A CLIENT AT MY PLACE OF BUSINESS AND SHE FALLS DOWN THE STEPS AND BREAKS A LEG. DOES SHE HAVE TO SUE ME TO COLLECT UNDER MY POLICY?

Most liability policies have a provision called medical payments that provides payment (up to a specified limit) of medical bills for injuries to third parties (persons other than yourself or your employees). If a client fell down the steps and had $1,000,000 worth of medical bills, your insurance company would be able to pay those bills even if the client did not institute a suit against you.

## WHAT IF MY CLIENT'S MEDICAL BILLS EXCEEDED MY POLICY LIMIT?

If the client does not want to sue you and is willing to work out an arrangement for reimbursement for her medical expenses, the insurance company may pay her medical bills if she is willing to sign a release.

The release should be prepared by your attorney (or you can use a form available in most good stationery stores). The release will indicate the date of the claim and the claimant's name and address, and contain language stating that in return for paying the bills, the claimant gives up all rights to bring suit against you.

## WILL MY POLICY PAY NO MATTER WHO'S AT FAULT ON A THIRD-PARTY CLAIM?

Not usually. The insurance company will investigate to see if you were negligent in the operation of your business: for instance, if your carpeting wasn't tacked down properly, if there was a crack in the sidewalk, or if a rack fell off the wall.

## WHAT IS PROPERTY DAMAGE LIABILITY?

Property damage liability pays for damage to property due to your negligence, or caused by products you manufacture, distribute, or sell.

## ARE THERE OTHER LIABILITY COVERAGES THAT I SHOULD BE LOOKING FOR UNDER MY CASUALTY-INSURANCE PROGRAM?

There are coverages called auto non-ownership and higher car coverage. Non-ownership is important if you have employees who use their personal cars for business.

For instance, a friend of mine who owns a clothing store sent an employee to the bank in the employee's own car to cash some business checks. On the way back to the store, the employee lost control of his vehicle and crashed through the window of a furniture store. There was severe damage to the building and its contents and bodily injury to customers. The store and the customers brought suit against the driver—and against the clothing store because the employee was on business time and using the car for business purposes. The costs of the suit were covered because the clothing-store owner had an auto non-ownership policy.

## WHAT IS HIGHER CAR COVERAGE?

Higher car coverage pertains to vehicles you rent on a short-term basis for business purposes, and provides excess coverage over that provided by the rental company.

## DO I NEED SEPARATE PROPERTY-INSURANCE AND CASUALTY-INSURANCE POLICIES?

No. Most small businesses would be eligible for a package policy that combines the property section and liability section. This is usually the best way to purchase your insurance. The package policy will have two or three sections, one for property you own, another for third-party liability, and possibly an inland marine section.

## WHAT IS INLAND MARINE COVERAGE?

The term "inland marine" refers to policies that provide coverage for such diverse items as fine arts, golf equipment, contractor's equipment, tools, and so on. Inland marine policies usually offer extremely broad coverage on property that is portable and valuable.

## WHAT KIND OF PACKAGE POLICY SHOULD I REQUEST FROM MY AGENT?

Your insurance agent should learn about your business and propose to you the type of policy that offers the best coverages at competitive premiums. You should thoroughly review the coverages proposed by your agent and look for any gaps in coverage. Examine not only what is covered, but understand what is excluded by the policy.

## WHAT IS A BUSINESSOWNERS POLICY?

The insurance industry developed a businessowners policy to provide comprehensive coverage for a small business in one policy. A businessowners policy provides property and liability coverage in one policy. It can be tailored to your individual needs by adding or subtracting coverages such as theft, plate-glass insurance, fidelity, accounts receivable, etc. Businessowners policies may not be appropriate for your firm because of the nature of your business or the need for specialized coverages that are not available under the businessowners program.

## I SELL ICE CREAM AT THE BEACH. IS THERE ANY PROVISION FOR GREATER COVERAGE DURING THE SUMMER?

Another addition to the businessowners policy is "peak season" coverage. The businessowners policy provides an automatic increase in your property limits of 24 percent to cover seasonal increases in your merchandise at no additional cost. The policy does insist that you insure your property for 100 percent of its replacement value during the remainder of the year to qualify for this coverage.

## WHAT OTHER TYPE OF BUSINESS POLICIES SHOULD I BE AWARE OF AFTER I HAVE CONTRACTED FOR MY PROPERTY AND LIABILITY INSURANCE?

You might want to have commercial automobile coverage. Coverage for commercial autos would be similar to personal auto coverage in that you would need a limit for bodily injury and property damage, as well as collision and comprehension deductibles (although the age and value of the vehicle would have to be taken into consideration). You would also want to purchase underinsurance and uninsurance coverage and medical payments.

Normally a commercially written auto policy is much more expensive than a personal policy. You should consult with your CPA to see whether it is more economical (i.e., for tax purposes) to insure the vehicle personally or in the business name.

## HOW MUCH WOULD THE DIFFERENCE BE BETWEEN COMMERCIAL AND PERSONAL AUTO INSURANCE?

In areas such as New York or New Jersey you could be paying two or three times the price to have the auto insured under a commercial name. A commercial policy takes into account that the car would be used more often and that more people usually have access to a vehicle used for business purposes.

## I AM PLANNING TO OPEN A RESTAURANT. IS THERE ANY ADDITIONAL COVERAGE OTHER THAN THOSE ALREADY MENTIONED THAT I SHOULD BE AWARE OF?

If you plan to serve liquor to your customers, you may need liquor-law legal liability coverage, which will protect you in case a customer consumes too much alcohol and gets into a car accident or causes injury to other people.

## I BOUGHT A PERSONAL UMBRELLA POLICY TO PROTECT MY PERSONAL ASSETS. IS THERE ALSO AN UMBRELLA POLICY AVAILABLE FOR MY BUSINESS?

Yes, there is, although it is a little more expensive than your personal policy. This type of policy would provide coverage over your existing liability limits as written under your general liability policy and your auto policy.

For instance, suppose you have a $1,000,000 limit per occurrence under your general liability policy, and a $1,000,000 limit under your auto, bodily injury, and property damage coverages, and you purchase an additional $1,000,000 umbrella policy. If you are sued for $2,000,000 due to an auto accident, injury on your premises, products liability, or any peril that was covered under your existing basic policies, an umbrella policy would provide ample coverage.

\*   \*   \*

## I OPERATE A SMALL BUSINESS OUT OF MY HOME. DO I NEED INSURANCE COVERAGE?

Generally, there are exclusions in your homeowners policy that pertain to business pursuits, or in some cases that limit the amount of income you can earn under a commercial venture from your home. If it's more than a hobby, you should be discussing separate coverage with your agent.

## WHAT TYPE OF COVERAGE SHOULD I BE DISCUSSING?

If you have outsiders coming to your home to discuss business or to buy products, you might need a commercial liability policy.

## DOES MY HOMEOWNERS POLICY EXTEND TO COVER BUSINESS PROPERTY IN MY HOME?

A homeowners policy provides a limited amount of business property coverage. The amount and types vary from company to company, so you should contact your insurance agent if you operate a business from your home or have business property stored there.

## WHAT ABOUT FAX MACHINES, ANSWERING MACHINES, AND TELEPHONES?

Property that is primarily used in a business would be subject to the limitations found in your homeowners policy. You should keep in mind that property purchased in a business name would alert the insurance company to the possibility of it being business property and be subject to any policy limitations.

## STATUTORY INSURANCE

## WHAT IS STATUTORY COVERAGE?

Statutory coverage is mandatory coverage required by the state or government, such as workers' compensation and short-term disability benefits. Most states require you to cover an employee for job-related injuries or illness.

## WHAT IS WORKERS' COMPENSATION? WHAT ARE THE BENEFITS OF WORKERS' COMPENSATION?

Workers'-compensation insurance provides statutory benefits to employees due to work-related accidents or illness. Benefits include all reasonable medical bills, loss of income, and lump-sum awards based upon the nature and extent of the injury or sickness.

The benefits vary by state. Some states have limits for medical benefits, while others offer unlimited coverage. Awards also vary. States such as New York and New Jersey have schedules, based upon a multiple of the employees' earnings, which indicate what they will pay.

## ONCE WORKERS' COMPENSATION TAKES CARE OF THE EMPLOYEE, AM I OFF THE HOOK?

Workers'-compensation insurance generally prohibits an employee from suing his or her employer. The exception is where the employer is grossly negligent.

For example, suppose you are working in a factory and are exposed to toxic chemicals that the employer knows will cause permanent injury. The employer has done nothing to protect you from the exposure or warn you as to the long-term effects. The injuries that result are compensable under workers' compensation; however, in this case you may want to sue your employer citing gross negligence.

## AS AN EMPLOYEE, WHAT DO I NEED TO KNOW ABOUT WORKERS' COMPENSATION?

You should make sure your employer carries compensation insurance. Employers are required by law to display a posting notice informing employees of the existence of workers'-compensation insurance, the name and policy number of the company providing the coverage, and how to file a claim.

## ARE ACCIDENTS THE ONLY THING THAT WOULD BE COVERED UNDER WORKERS'-COMPENSATION POLICY? SUPPOSE MY EMPLOYEE HAS A HEART ATTACK ON THE WAY TO OR FROM THE OFFICE OR GOING TO THE BANK?

Workers' compensation normally applies to job-related injuries. However, many claims have been settled recently for off-premises injuries related to the job. For example, an employee might indicate he was working too hard or working too many hours, and under extreme pressure, and that's what caused his heart attack.

In some states, having an accident while traveling to and from work might be deemed an on-the-job injury because the employee would not have been using his car or would not have been commuting had he not been going to work.

## ARE MY EMPLOYEES COVERED IF THEY ARE EXPOSED TO TOXIC SUBSTANCES AND DEVELOP A LONG-TERM ILLNESS?

The employee would be covered for workers'-compensation benefits. It is sometimes difficult to determine the cause of an illness that doesn't manifest itself for some time. For example, it took doctors years to determine that asbestos exposure causes long-term illness, disability, and death.

## IT IS SOMETIMES DIFFICULT TO DETERMINE WHETHER SOMEONE IS AN EMPLOYEE OR AN INDEPENDENT CONTRACTOR. HOW IS THIS DETERMINED?

In many states, the difference between an independent contractor and an employee is a gray area of the law.

Generally, independent contractors are those individuals who are self-employed and provide services without the employer's direct control. Where control is exercised, the courts and the IRS often find there is an employer-employee relationship. It has sometimes happened that an individual is found to be an independent contractor for tax purposes, but is found to be an employee under insurance law.

Examples of independent contractors are real-estate agents working in a large office, a painter you employ to paint the inside of your store, or the lawn service that takes care of your yard. However, if you hire someone to paint your store and provide them with the paint, brushes, drop cloths, ladders, etc., and frequently monitor their performance, you probably have an employee. If you have any question, you should check with your attorney or accountant, as the definition of an employee is different in every state.

## HOW DO I DETERMINE WHETHER SOMEONE WHO WORKS FOR ME IS UNDER MY DIRECTION OR CONTROL?

The criteria for determining this include: Does she perform duties assigned by you? Is she subject to dismissal? Do you furnish the materials, tools, and equipment necessary to do the job? Do you set the time and place for her employment? There are some twenty different areas in the Internal Revenue Manual that the IRS uses to classify individuals. Insurance law generally follows the IRS, but as stated above, in certain situations it may be possible for an individual to be considered an independent contractor for the IRS and an employee under insurance law. When in doubt, consult a qualified attorney or accountant.

## DOES THE FACT THAT I PAY THE EMPLOYEE UNDER A 1099 OR A W2 FORM—ONE BEING AS AN EMPLOYED INDIVIDUAL, THE OTHER AS AN INDEPENDENT CONTRACTOR— HAVE ANY BEARING ON WHETHER HE IS AN EMPLOYEE OR NOT?

Not usually. Providing a 1099 is not the deciding factor, but only one of a number of "tests" the courts may look at.

## WHAT DO I DO IF I'M NOT SURE WHETHER SOMEONE I'M HIRING IS TRULY AN INDEPENDENT CONTRACTOR?

Call your insurance agent or the state workers'-compensation board nearest you and give them all the facts. They should be able to guide you.

*   *   *

## IF I HAVE AN INDEPENDENT CONTRACTOR COME TO MY HOME OR BUSINESS, AND HE GIVES ME A CERTIFICATE OF INSURANCE SHOWING THAT HE HAS COVERAGE FOR WORKERS' COMPENSATION AND GENERAL LIABILITY, DOES THAT MEAN I WON'T BE LIABLE?

In most instances, yes. However, many states have what is called a "safe place to work" law, which requires you to provide a safe environment for any workers. Should the independent contractor allege gross negligence on your part for not providing safe working conditions, he may be able to bring suit against you.

Keep in mind that not everyone who is an independent contractor carries insurance. Most independents are individuals working on a tight budget that may not have room for liability and workers'-compensation premiums. If you're hiring someone to do potentially "dangerous" work (using ladders, climbing onto the roof, etc.) you should only contract with those individuals who carry insurance and furnish you with a certificate prior to the start of a job.

## WHAT HAPPENS IF I HAVE AN EMPLOYEE OR INDEPENDENT CONTRACTOR WHO BECOMES INJURED WHILE DOING WORK FOR ME?

The law requires that all injuries to your employees be reported to workers' compensation promptly (generally within ten days).

Injuries to independent contractors should also be reported promptly, both to workers' compensation and to your general liability carrier. Attach any certificates of insurance you may have, and indicate in the report that the injured party was an independent contractor. Your independent insurance agent will help you with filing the proper forms.

## IS THERE OTHER STATUTORY COVERAGE OTHER THAN WORKERS' COMPENSATION?

Several states require you to have a short-term disability policy for your employees. Presently only four states—New York, New Jersey, California, and Rhode Island—mandate this coverage.

## DO I, AS THE EMPLOYER, PAY FOR THIS DISABILITY INSURANCE?

Employers can deduct a portion of the premium from their employees' paycheck every week to offset the cost of the disability insurance. The amount varies by state. New York allows a deduction of a maximum of one half of 1 percent of weekly wages up to a maximum of sixty cents weekly; Rhode Island allows employers to deduct 1.2 percent of the first $9,800 of annual wages. Check with your insurance agent or accountant to determine what the maximum deductions are in your area.

## WHAT TYPE OF COVERAGE DOES MY DISABILITY INSURANCE PROVIDE TO MY EMPLOYEES?

Usually disability benefits cover off-the-job injury or sickness, and it reimburses the employee for a percentage of his lost wages for a specified period of time.

## SUPPOSE AN EMPLOYEE OF MINE GOT SICK AND HE WAS EARNING $300 A WEEK. WHAT MIGHT HE LOOK FORWARD TO IN REIMBURSEMENT?

In New York, he would get 50 percent of his salary to a maximum of $170 a week for a twenty-six-week period, starting on the eighth day of disability. Check with your insurance agent or accountant in other states.

## CAN I AS AN EMPLOYER PAY MY EMPLOYEE WAGES WHILE HE WAS INJURED AND GET REIMBURSED FROM THE STATUTORY DISABILITY CARRIER?

You can continue paying the employee and be reimbursed directly by the disability carrier. You must notify the carrier that you are paying the salary and want reimbursement.

# CONCLUSION

# TEN KEY POINTS ABOUT YOU, INSURANCE, AND YOUR INSURANCE AGENT

## 1. YOU CAN, AND MUST, TAKE RESPONSIBILITY FOR YOUR OWN INSURANCE "HEALTH" AND WELL-BEING.

This doesn't mean you have to become your own insurance agent or make all your decisions by yourself. It does mean that you have to make informed choices about the insurance agents, companies, and policies you choose.

## 2. STAND UP FOR YOUR RIGHT TO ASK QUESTIONS.

You have to be persistent. An agent may be busy, or may not be prepared to answer all your questions. However, insurance agents are taught to ask questions— you may have to remind your agent that he is not the only one who can ask them.

## 3. THE ONLY WAY TO GET THE INFORMATION YOU NEED IS BY ASKING QUESTIONS.

Don't be afraid to admit you don't know. Great inventions and scientific discoveries were made by people who "didn't know." They admitted to the world they didn't know all the answers; then they asked questions, questions, and more questions, until they found the answers they needed.

### 4. DISCOVER YOUR OPTIONS.

Options give you control over any situation. Never do anything (or refrain from doing anything) just because your insurance agent said so. Find out what your choices are, then make your decision.

### 5. KNOWLEDGE REDUCES FEAR AND ANXIETY.

It's not what we know that scares us, it's what we don't know. Decisions that involve present and future finances can be very stressful, for yourself and for your family. You don't want to waste your strength and energy on imaginary or unnecessary concerns.

### 6. NEVER ASSUME.

Don't assume that you have all the information you need. An agent may have given similar policy descriptions to 2,000 other people—but forget to give you one vital piece of information. Don't assume something is right for you just because an agent says it's so. Think about what you're doing, and make the agent think as well!

### 7. DON'T ACCEPT AN EASY ANSWER. PROBE AND CLARIFY.

Little children do this automatically. Answer a question and they'll come back with a "why?" every time. You should do the same. You want to be sure you understand everything that's going on, and that you are getting your money's worth for any services rendered.

### 8. AN INSURANCE AGENT IS JUST A HUMAN BEING.

No matter how intimidating, aggressive, or knowledge-able she may seem, an agent really is just a human being. That means she can make human mistakes. She can also be warm, sympathetic, and understanding. Let her know what you need, and how she can help you.

## 9. BUILD A ONE-ON-ONE RELATIONSHIP WITH YOUR AGENT.

You don't have to become best friends. Asking questions sets up an immediate rapport with the agent. The agent's attitudes, as well as his answers, will give you important clues about his background and personality— and help you make a choice that is right for you.

Your questioning attitude lets him know that you're special, and that you intend to establish a partnership with him concerning all your insurance dealings.

## 10. ASK SMART QUESTIONS. ASK SMART QUESTIONS. ASK MORE SMART QUESTIONS.

If you want to know more about Dorothy Leeds's speeches, seminars, and audiocassette programs, please call or write to:

Dorothy Leeds, President
Organizational Technologies Inc.
800 West End Avenue, Suite 10A
New York, NY 10025
(212) 864-2424

Her Positive Action Cassette Learning Programs are the following:

*Smart Questions: The Key to Sales Success.* This unique and proven program will help you improve your questions to solve the mystery of the decision-making process, uncover the right information in the right way at the right time, practice surefire ways to answer objections, and close the sale.

*PowerSpeak: The Complete Guide to Persuasive Public Speaking and Presenting.* You can easily become a powerful and persuasive presenter by following Dorothy Leeds's proven PowerSpeak method.

*The Motivational Manager: How to Get Top Performance from Your Staff.* Being an excellent manager is the best way to get ahead. With this motivational program you will discover your strengths and weaknesses, how to hire, coach, train, motivate, and lots more.

*People Reading: Strategies for Engineering Better Relationships in Business.* Gain a huge career advantage by influencing others and achieving results through reading the unique differences in people.

# INDEX